THE COURT OF THE MEDICI

THE COURT OF THE MEDICI

George Pottinger

CROOM HELM LONDON
ROWMAN AND LITTLEFIELD TOTOWA N.J.

© 1978 G. Pottinger
Croom Helm Ltd, 2-10 St John's Road, London SW11

British Library Cataloguing in Publication Data

Pottinger, George
    The Court of the Medici.
    1. Medici family
    I. Title
    945'.51   DG737.42

    ISBN 0–85664–605–9

First published in the United States 1977
by Rowman and Littlefield, Totowa, N.J.

ISBN 0-8476-6024-9

Printed in Great Britain by Biddles Ltd, Guildford, Surrey

CONTENTS

For M.D.A.

FOREWORD

Interest in the Medici waxes and wanes, but there is no shortage of learned monographs on various aspects of the family's mystique. This book is addressed to the general reader. It attempts to set out how the Medici acquired their authority: how they exercised their influence: and how they generated and fostered enthusiasm for the arts. Some of the themes which emerge — autocratic rule within a seemingly popular constitution, and the role of state patronage — are surprisingly topical, and modern parallels are identified.

After the death of Lorenzo in 1492 the Medici were driven from power, and those who returned to the city after the interregnum were of a different stamp. The book accordingly concentrates on the family's activities in fifteenth century Florence. Savonarola provides a grim postscript.

Medici politics are interwoven with the relationship between the family and the artists, scholars and writers who formed their circle. The lives and work of Angelo Poliziano and Pico della Mirandola — who has attracted less attention than he deserves — are given some prominence. I cannot, however, match the expertise of many who have studied all the different facets of the Florentine scene, and I am glad to acknowledge my debt to those whose treatises I have read.

Friends have helped in the preparation of the text. The distinguished Roman lawyer Gianni Manca and his wife Paola — in whose house I wrote the first outline — advised on the Italian ambience, as did his colleague Mario Beltramo. Ian Parsons read the manuscript and pointed to improvements. L. Pompa of the Philosophy Department of Edinburgh University contributed much to the chapter on Pico: and my brother Don Pottinger made many pungent observations on the sections dealing with the Florentine artists. The staff of the National Library of Scotland were, as always, keen to assist. I hope that others whom I consulted, too numerous to mention, will accept my grateful thanks.

Without my wife's research and patient understanding 'The Court of the Medici' would not have been possible.

Balsham, 1977

THE MEDICI FAMILY TREE

XVth Century Genealogy

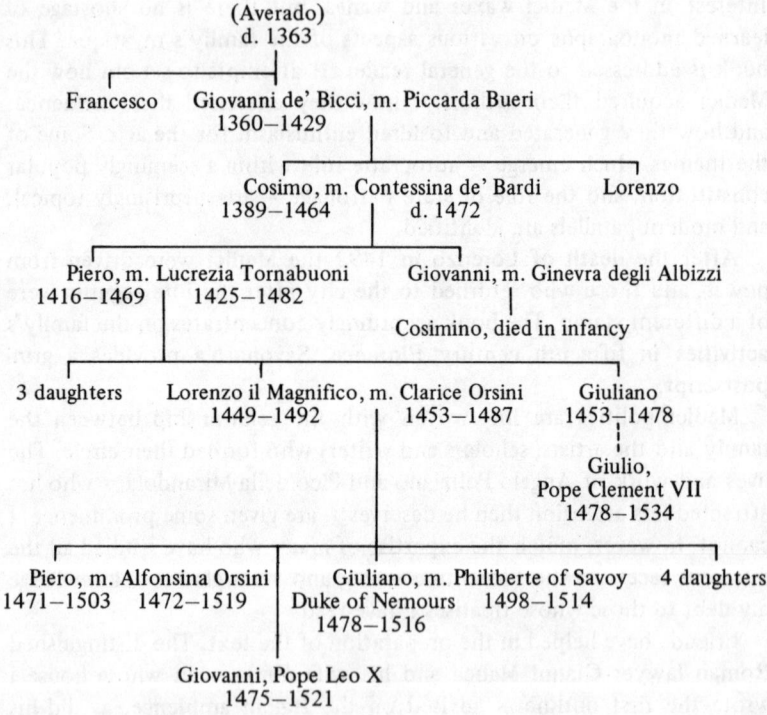

(Averado)
d. 1363

Francesco — Giovanni de' Bicci, m. Piccarda Bueri
1360–1429

Cosimo, m. Contessina de' Bardi   Lorenzo
1389–1464   d. 1472

Piero, m. Lucrezia Tornabuoni   Giovanni, m. Ginevra degli Albizzi
1416–1469   1425–1482

Cosimino, died in infancy

3 daughters   Lorenzo il Magnifico, m. Clarice Orsini   Giuliano
1449–1492   1453–1487   1453–1478

Giulio,
Pope Clement VII
1478–1534

Piero, m. Alfonsina Orsini   Giuliano, m. Philiberte of Savoy   4 daughters
1471–1503   1472–1519   Duke of Nemours   1498–1514
1478–1516

Giovanni, Pope Leo X
1475–1521

Headship of the Medici Family

Giovanni de' Bicci	1400–1429
Cosimo	1429–1464
Piero	1464–1469
Lorenzo il Magnifico	1469–1492
Piero	1492–1494
Interregnum	1494–1512

INTRODUCTION

Roads in Tuscany ride on crests and ridges. Tuscan towns and villages cluster like bee-hives round the tops of hills. The reason is not hard to find. The highways and buildings have been sited not for convenience — roads on the heights are windswept and difficult to maintain and the steep slopes of hills greatly aggravate town planning — but for security. The traveller in fifteenth-century Italy who was tempted to take an easier route along the bottom of a valley was very likely to meet an ambuscade. Enemies could more easily attack on low-lying ground, as the citizens of villages which could be dominated from surrounding eminences soon learned. So the Italians, and in Tuscany the contours are very suitable for this purpose, built their roads and houses on the tops of hills.

Violence, or the threat of violence, is never far below the surface or life in Italy, particularly during the first Medici period with which we are concerned, from Giovanni de' Bicci to the death of Lorenzo the Magnificent in 1492. Luigi Barzini has written recently,

Italians first of all fear sudden and violent death. The vigorous passions of a turbulent and restless people are always ready to flare up unexpectedly like hot coals under the ashes. Italy is a blood-stained country. Almost every day of the year jealous husbands kill their adulterous wives and their lovers; about as many wives kill their adulterous husbands and their mistresses; fathers or older brothers kill the seducers of defenceless and guileless virgins; virgins kill the men trying to rape them; desperate young lovers commit suicide together in pairs, or separately one at a time. This steady massacre, inspired by love, which has been going on for centuries, has surely cost more lives than the many pestilences and catastrophes which have ravaged the country, and the wars fought on Italian soil.[1]

If this is still true today, how much greater was the prospect of sudden death five centuries ago when Papal plots, and the rivalries of city states and powerful factions with paid mercenaries roaming at large, had to be added to the more personal problems described by Barzini. While the Italians have always been much addicted to violent solutions, they are not singularly skilful at carrying them out. Other European countries would coldly arrange for assassinations to be undertaken by one or two

11

professionals, but in Italy the employment of a large *posse* was more customary. The result was that either the victim escaped — the Quattrocento is full of bungled plots — or that the actual mayhem was very messy.

It will be one of the aims of this book to demonstrate how, against this background of violence, sporadic rebellion and wars with foreign powers, Florence in the time of the Medici saw the first and finest flowering of the spirit of the Renaissance. During most of this period the population of Florence numbered about one hundred thousand. Not all of these had rights as citizens and not all were even remotely affected by the New Learning. But a surprising number were, as artists, sculptors or architects and many more as craftsmen. Florence of the time was, at least in theory, deliberately democratic and, while it is true that some of the leading families could manipulate the system to their own advantage, any man of ability had a chance of reaching a position of influence. Bartolommeo Scala, the miller's son, became Chancellor of Florence; Marsilio Ficino, whose father was a physician, was put in charge of the Platonic Academy; and Angelo Poliziano rose from the most impoverished circumstances to become the intimate friend of the Magnificent.

Poliziano's name occurs frequently in these pages and some account of his origins and his first approach to Lorenzo will serve as an introduction. He was born Agnolo (or Angelo) Ambrogini and the name Poliziano, by which he is commonly known, comes from a Latinised form of his birthplace at Montepulciano — Mons Politianus. Montepulciano, which lies almost seventy miles to the south-east of Florence, swarms round the top of one of the hills that point the Tuscan countryside. From a distance it looks like a painting by Fra Angelico. Its fame rests on three things — the wine it produces, the Church of San Biagio nearby and its association with Poliziano.

The wine is too good to ignore. The best vintage from Montepulciano is a dry, nutty-flavoured red with a distinctive flavour unusual in most Italian wines. It is sold mostly from one cantina whose cellars — pilgrims are encouraged to walk through them — make a cool, musty-scented contrast to the arid air outside. And, if the bouquet of the wine does not compare with the great wines of France, the appointments of the cantina can emulate the *caves* of Burgundy. Montepulciano is best drunk at a café table in the piazza in the centre of the town or on the terrace which forms a belvedere beside the cantina itself. In the latter event, the second or third glass will induce some vinous reflections on the endless series of cypress trees running up the smaller hills which lie below.

How do they preserve their absurdly mathematical appearance? What Tuscan princeling planted them? Were the Tuscans the heirs of the Etruscans? Is this not the same scene that the young Ambrogini looked on much later? One last word on the local wines: Montepulciano travels and bottles can be borne away in triumph.

The fields surrounding the Church of San Biagio are a favourite place for visitors. There is a panoramic view to the north and a slightly decaying atmosphere which induces a remembrance of things past, a feeling of having been there before. The Church has for long been cherished by architects and historians as a good example of the work of the elder San Gallo. Today it provokes two reflections. First, how was the comparatively small population of Montepulciano in the Medici period – reckoned in a few hundreds – able to subscribe to building a church the size of a ship? It may be defended as an act of piety; as an exercise in social economics it is more redolent of exaction than prudence. Second, although for those brought up in a mainly Gothic tradition it is often difficult to contemplate the work of many Italian architects with anything more than a detached interest in their wilder extravagances, San Biagio has a charm that is immediately apparent. A massive, square building in the form of a Greek cross surmounted by a cupola with a baptistery still unfinished (because of priestly peculation or the belated indignation of the local worshippers), its austere lines and unusual lack of ostentation are appealing.

But San Biagio lies outside the walls: and our main concern is inside. There are a number of architectural features of note – for example, the Chiesa di Sant' Agostino designed by Michelozzo in a very Florentine style with a wonderfully decorative doorway, and the Palazzo Tarugi, probably planned by Vignola. Of more immediate interest, half way up one of the narrow streets leading to the summit of the town, there is a plaque on the wall identifying a house as the birthplace of Poliziano:

Angelo di Benedetto Ambrogini
    In queste case
Che poi dal mutato cognome della famiglia
    Si dissero de' cini
    Vide la luce
Vi passo' tra pericoli la fanciullezza
E fatto orfano da crudeli nemici
Giovinetto e povero le lasciava
Per rivederle famoso col nome di Poliziano
    Sotto il quale

Salutato rinnovatore della Toscana poesia all' Italiana
E degli umani studi all' universale civilta
Lo festeggiammo con solenne commemorazione
Noi suoi concittadini
Nel Luglio dell' anno MDCCCLXXV
CCCXXI dalla nascita.

The house, an unremarkable fourteenth-century building, is still occupied and the street is called the Via Poliziano. Apart from this and a fairly dilapidated communal building bearing the inscription 'Teatro Poliziano', there is now no trace of his family, his works or his residence in Montepulciano.

Angelo was the eldest of the five children of Benedetto Ambrogini and his wife Antonia Salimbeni. The family enjoyed a modest way of life. Benedetto, who was a doctor of law, had served his term as Gonfaloniere, or chief magistrate, which denotes some standing in the community; but, in one of the feuds common in Renaissance Italy, he was murdered by his enemies in 1464.

Angelo was then only ten years old and his widowed mother, faced with looking after five small children, took the prudent course of despatching him to Florence to live with a relation there. Although the next few years were to be hard (his uncle's dwelling was poor and there was no money to spare) Angelo was fortunate in his mother's decision. Florence was to be his home for most of the rest of his life and, though he could not have appreciated it, he had arrived at the right town at the right time. Cosimo de' Medici died about the same time as Angelo came to Florence. The city had benefited greatly from his peaceful administration over the last thirty years. Cosimo had no great love for violence; he does not seem to have had the *dono di corragio:* certainly he did not cut a very heroic figure when he was imprisoned by the Albizzi in 1433, and he took great pains to ensure that he was not again subjected to physical danger. The first five years after Angelo arrived saw a fallow, peaceful time under the rule of Piero il Gottoso, and the real Medici springtime was already starting under the influence of Cosimo's young grandsons, Lorenzo and Giuliano. Following a period of stable peace, it was a time of hope, expectation and frequent merriment.

For, by now, Florence was full of artists and their works. Ghiberti's gates were in position at the Baptistery of San Giovanni. Brunelleschi's Dome for the Cathedral of Santa Maria del Fiore had been completed about thirty years before and still excited astonishment and wonder. Donatello was still at work in his studio producing his monumental sculptures to serve as models for his contemporaries. Michelozzo had designed the new Medici town house and Luca della Robbia was busy in the factory he had founded turning out masterpieces in glazed terracotta made by his own process. Among painters, Masaccio, the first real genius of the Medici century, was dead but his influence inspired many of his successors. Those two remarkably unlike friars – Fra Angelico and Filippo Lippi – had brought Renaissance painting to new heights, and there were giants still to come. There were those who seemed able to practise all the arts – architecture, sculpture, painting, and music – like Verrocchio and Alberti. And, at a more mundane level, Florence had a great number of craftsmen working in precious metals, wood and leather, and there was a close relationship between craftsmen and artists. Both benefited from studying the antiques, manuscripts and treasures which the Medici family were collecting from all their outposts throughout Europe to enrich the city.

Although the streets were dirty and refuse frequently had to be burned, and although the windows were covered with treated vellum, it was a surprisingly comfortable and civilised town. Baths were an unusual addiction of the fifteenth-century Florentines – in their houses and at mineral springs where 'the cure' was early in fashion; a fashion led by Lucrezia Tornabuoni, the wife of Piero de' Medici. A great deal was spent on furniture and furnishings and the interest in dress and entertainments, raised to a new pitch in Lorenzo's time, was already intense. Throughout strolled the Florentines. As a rule they were taller than most other Italians and they tended to covet fair hair. They had the long noses which can be seen still in their portraits and in their twentieth-century descendants.

Angelo was not endowed with any great physical beauty. Judging by the figure of him which appears in the portrait by Ghirlandaio in the Sassetti Chapel of the Church of Santa Trinita, he had a slightly menacing appearance with a large, hooked nose and a cast in one eye. His hair is black and long; there is an impression of intellectual strength, but not of kindness; and there is no trace of elegance.

It seems likely that Angelo realised early that, if he was not to spend the rest of his life as a manual worker in the Via Saturnia or some other humble quarter, he would have to make his own way by means of his studies; he could then seek preferment, either by admission to one of the holy orders, or by gaining the patronage of one of the wealthy families. Meanwhile, he applied himself with such diligence to the instruction given by his teachers at the school of the Compagnia di Dottrina that he soon earned a reputation for precocity as a scholar.

Latin and Greek were still the main subjects — although the native Tuscan tongue was, under Lorenzo's influence, to become more respectable as a literary medium — and Angelo's first achievements were in writing Latin letters and epigrams. Then he began on a task sufficient to alarm even the most learned of scholars — the translation of Homer's *Iliad* into Latin hexameters. He had finished Book II when he was only sixteen and decided to send it to Lorenzo, who had only recently succeeded Piero as head of the Medici family. It would be interesting to know what prompted him to take this courageous step. Was it the wise advice of one of his preceptors, confidence in his own ability, or a realisation that only Lorenzo could help him? In any event, he addressed Lorenzo with a letter written in the terms which were common when approaching a prospective patron:

> Magnificent Lorenzo, to whom heaven has given charge of the city and the State, first citizen of Florence, doubly crowned with bays lately for war in Santa Croce amid the acclamations of the people and for poetry on account of the sweetness of your verses, give ear to me who drinking at Greek sources am striving to set Homer into Latin metre. This second book which I have translated (you know we have the first by Messer Carlo d' Arezzo) comes to you and timidly crosses your threshold. If you welcome it I propose to offer to you all the *Iliad*. It rests with you, who can, to help the poet. I desire no other muse or other Gods but only you; by your help I can do that of which the ancients would not have been ashamed. May it please you therefore at your leisure to give audience to Homer. The young translator, if assailed by a Zoilus, commends himself to you.
>
> AGNOLO POLIZIANO, 1470.[2]

The response was quick and generous. Lorenzo sent for Poliziano, gave him accommodation in the Medici Palace and allowed him to continue his work there. He was provided with badly-needed new clothes and sent to study at the Studio Fiorentino under Marsilio Ficino and the leading classical scholars of the day. At that time Poliziano can scarcely have foreseen his future career as an intimate friend of Lorenzo, a career clouded only by his eventual quarrel with Lorenzo's wife, or that most of the rest of his life would be spent in the company of Lorenzo's wits and humanists. Nor could he have appreciated that he had approached the ruling member of the most remarkable family produced by Renaissance Italy.

Notes

1. Luigi Barzini, *The Italians* (Hamish Hamilton, London, 1964).
2. Janet Ross, *Lives of the Early Medici as told in Their Correspondence* (Chatto and Windus, London, 1910).

1 THE COUNTING-HOUSE

Much has been written about the Medici but attitudes to, and understanding of, their careers change with each generation. Succeeding decades are also able to call on ever-increasing resources unearthed by research scholars who are attracted by the magnetic quality of the great bell which Florentines sounded in times of crisis. In this and the following chapters an attempt is made to bring together the fruits of recent studies; to reassess in lay terms the progress of the early Medici from Giovanni de' Bicci to the death of Lorenzo; and to identify the nature of the Medici mystique, both as it affected Poliziano and as it appeals to us.

As far back as they can be identified, the Medici were of good middle-class stock. Lest this may seem too facile a definition, there are no records to show that they were poor, and for most of the fifteenth century they were very rich. Cosimo was much the wealthiest citizen of Florence, and his fortune passed without any decimating estate duty to his son and grandson. But, though they were ambitious for power, the Medici never aspired to noble status. To do so overtly would have been dangerous in Florence where attempts at ostentation or the merest sign of *hubris* led at once to accusations. So it was not only from humility, but also from a sense of self-preservation, that the Medici as a family always allied themselves with the citizens *(popolani)* against the nobles *(grandi)*. A relation, Salvestro de' Medici had been Gonfaloniere of Justice during the earlier historic revolt by the weavers and dyers *(ciompi)* in 1378. After the passing of the Ordinamenti della Giustizia in 1293, the old nobility had been excluded from holding magisterial office. From then on a member of the patrician families had to enter the ranks of the people and matriculate into one of the guilds *(arti)* if he wanted to exercise authority in the State. This path was not always made easy; a strange paradox of social equality, but it shows that peerages could be renounced more than four hundred years ago.

Florence claimed to be a democratic republic and, in most respects, it was more democratic than any of the other Italian city States, but the power of participating in elections was confined to those enrolled as burghers. One of the most valuable gifts that Lorenzo could bestow on the humanists who came from elsewhere in Italy to make their home in Florence was to make them citizens.

The Medici were always concerned with banking and commercial enterprises, but there is no satisfactory explanation of the origin of their name or of the coat-of-arms, the famous five balls. It has been alleged that 'Medici' must have referred to an original profession of medicine, but the two probable sources of this legend are both spurious. First, Cosimo de' Medici chose as his patron saints San Cosimo and San Damian, the two doctor saints, and introduced references to them in pictures painted in his honour: but this seems more like a punning device — and the Florentines loved puns — than a tenable proposition. Secondly, much later, the wits of Paris, who never took kindly to Catherine de' Medici and affected to despise her bourgeois origins, invented a story that the Medici were originally poor apothecaries and the family arms, the *palle,* or balls, represented chemists' pills. This seems most unlikely. Is it credible that, at a time when passions were roused at the height of the Pazzi conspiracy and the whole fabric of the State was at risk, the Medici supporters, answering the conspirators' cry of 'Popolo e liberta' with a loyal shout of 'Vivano le palle', were invoking the help of chemists' pills?

Nor does there appear to be any connection between the red roundels (heraldically, *torteaux)* in the Medici coat-of-arms and the three golden balls familiar to those who have had to pledge a gold watch or a piece of jewellery at the pawnbroker's. A more probable explanation is that throughout Europe pawnbrokers used the three golden roundels (*Bezants*) because they had for long been recognised as the symbol of money. It would have been intriguing to find a usurer as the Medici progenitor deploying and multiplying his talents of gold; but no such figure exists. So the Medici name and the heraldic significance of their arms remains unexplained.

Long before the fifteenth century, Florence had become an essentially commercial city with merchant princes effectively in charge and an extensive foreign trade, especially with Western Europe. The principal trade was in wool, particularly after the Florentines began to buy wool in England as well as in Spain. Many of the better-known Florentine families were among the *mercanti* and owned warehouses. The roll includes the names of the Albizzi, Bardi, Capponi, Peruzzi, Pucci and Rinuccini families. The Medici were registered as members of the Guild of Cloth Makers (Calimala), and only later does their name appear in the Bankers' Guild (Arte del Cambio).

But the Italians were not only the principal merchants; they were also the principal bankers of the Middle Ages and the Renaissance. The most important customer of the Italian bankers was, inevitably, the

Church, and the flow of remittances from Rome was at least as important as trade contracts. The stability of local currencies depended in the last resort on the backing of the Holy See. Florentine banking was based on companies — extraordinarily like modern holding companies — with head-quarters in the city and a framework of branches overseas. Siena had for long been the main banking centre until, on the failure of the Gran Tavola of the Bonsignori in 1298, the more tenacious Florentines took their place. From 1300 to 1350 the leading Florentine bankers were the Bardi, Peruzzi and Acciaiuoli families. These three families, however, failed as bankers in the years around 1350. The cause of their failure is not entirely clear, but one contributory factor was that most of them had large outstanding loans to monarchs, especially Edward III of England who was as good at raising credit as he was evasive about repayment. For some time after them the Alberti got control of most of the accounts with Rome, but their supremacy did not last long. The Alberti were then replaced by the Medici, the Pazzi, the Rucellai and the Strozzi. Although the Medici family eventually captured the leading position, it is an odd and seldom remembered fact that they never became as big — as bankers — as the Bardi or the Peruzzi in the previous century. The crucial date in the history of the Medici bank is probably 1397 when the head of the family, Giovanni de' Bicci, decided to bring his head-quarters back from Rome to Florence. The Medici bank prospered in varying degrees from the turn of the century until the sequestration of the family estates in 1494. Expansion was steady until the death of Cosimo in 1464, but there was a gradual decline after the Pazzi conspiracy in 1478 — the watershed in Medici history — and Lorenzo's lack of real interest in banking as a way of life was a contributory factor in the subsequent attrition of their financial influence.

The period up to 1451 is amply documented in the Medici confi-dential ledgers *(libri segreti)*. Thereafter the evidence is to be found mainly in the correspondence which remains in fairly extensive form. It is clear from a perusal of the letters that in the second half of the century the branches were getting into trouble, branch managers were becoming less disciplined and the direction from the head of the Medici house was becoming less sure. All the melancholy signs of a great commercial organisation on the verge of breakdown were becoming apparent. It is ironic that, while the reputation of the Medici survives primarily because of their role in statecraft and as patrons of the arts, and while the found-ation of their power was their wealth derived from banking, nevertheless they never attracted a great degree of attention in their chosen pro-fession. From the time of Giovanni de' Bicci, however, the tax records show that they remained for the rest of the century the richest family in the city. As bankers they were not innovators and their success was mainly due to improving existing techniques, particularly under the strong grip of Cosimo.

Most of the leading Florentine families had some interest in the woollen industry and from 1402 at least the Medici family were financing a workshop *(bottega)* for the production of woollen cloth, and another similar partnership was formed in 1408. But although the Medici were merchant bankers in the true sense of the word, the actual staff employed was small. The Florentine banker would transact his business in a small room which had a table or counter, a few desks and an abacus on which the sums were done. There would seldom be more than half-a-dozen or so clerks in the accounting room. In 1402 the pay-roll of the Medici bank was no more than seventeen.

It may seem remarkable at first sight that the Florentine artists who depended so much on the favour of the Medici should not have recorded a banking transaction in progress; but, on reflection, it is not so strange. Contemporary church teaching was rigorously opposed to any form of usury — and the banker makes his money from the interest earned by the advance he grants to his customers. Various dialectical devices were used to escape from this dilemma; the principal one was to describe each banking transaction as a form of exchange in such a way that the capital and interest were not shown separately. It is significant that the guild of the Bankers, the Arte del Cambio, was called the Exchange Guild, and the bankers themselves were clearly concerned to practise their calling in decent obscurity.

The Medici made no attempt to conceal their banking origins. This would, in any event, have been an impossible task when large numbers of their fellow-citizens owed substantial sums to the bank and, at a higher level, the ability of the Medici to control large sums of money on call was an important element in Florence's foreign policy. There is, however, no sign that they did anything to emphasise their close connection with the counting-house. Of the Medici who ruled the family throughout the century, Giovanni de' Bicci and Cosimo were recognisably bankers above all else. Piero was a singularly bad banker and his first major banking transaction nearly precipitated his downfall. His son, Lorenzo, sought his many interests in very different fields.

The gradual capital appreciation of the Medici bank can be seen in the family's acquisition of property. The Medici reinvested their profits in the Mugello and the surrounding countryside, for example, at Poggio a Caiano where Lorenzo built his favourite villa. The careful upward trend of the family fortunes can also be identified in their successive marriages. The first Medici wives came from good Florentine families, but it was not long before subsequent generations aspired to unions with more noble families and, finally, the ruling families in Europe. (A precedent followed with some frequency by financiers since then.) But the Medici were careful to avoid any of the more irritating habits practised by the *nouveau riche*, for puffed-up pride was much despised in Florence long before Savonarola denounced it in theological terms.

There appears to have been an unusually detailed stocktaking in the Medici bank in 1441 following the death of Cosimo's brother. The accounts showed the balance in the possession of the bank as being approximately 74,000 florins. There were headquarters in Florence, branches in Rome and Venice, shares in partnerships at Ancona, Bruges and Genoa, and a number of industrial companies. The bank was still to spread its tentacles further with branches to be formed at Avignon, London and Milan, the London branch being set up five years later in 1446.

The Medici bank reached its peak in Cosimo's rule, largely due to his own inspiration and the helpful trading conditions at the time. Cosimo was good at personnel selection. He always found the right man for the job. He was good at delegation but kept a firm grip on his branch managers. Although much concerned with Florentine politics, and although he for long maintained a ruling position within the constitutional framework, his main interest was the management of the bank. Bearing in mind the poor communications throughout Europe, it was essential that delegation should be good and based on mutual confidence. This Cosimo achieved.

As merchants the Medici were interested in many varieties of trading enterprises. They dealt not only in wool but also in many other commodities such as spices and silks. Other entries in the Medici accounts show more recherché adventures. For example, in 1441 the branch in Venice was involved in buying ginger. The branch in Bruges took part in recruiting choir boys with high-pitched voices for the choir of San Giovanni Laterano in Rome. Medici agents throughout Europe had standing instructions to look for lost volumes and manuscripts of the classics. They were also interested in developing the valuable alum deposits which were found at Tolfa near Civitavecchia in 1460. Another discovery of alum near Volterra led the citizens of the town to revolt in 1470 against the Florentines who were exploiting the discovery. The punitive measures and the subsequent sack of Volterra by the forces sent under the command of the Duke of Urbino were often a matter of reproach against Lorenzo. The Medici were also interested in another mineral — the iron ore deposits on the Island of Elba.

It seems likely that they also sold wine by the bottle at the doors of their great houses, an endearing custom which survived for at least another three centuries. Tobias Smollett on a visit to the city in 1765 was surprised to note that, with all their pride, the nobles of Florence were humble enough to enter into partnership with shopkeepers and even to sell wine by retail. He recorded that in every palace or great house there was a little window fronting the street, provided with an iron knocker, over which hung an empty flask, by way of signpost.

Thither you send your servant to buy a bottle of wine. He knocks at the little wicket, which is opened immediately by a domestic, who supplies him with what he wants, and receives the money like the waiter of any other cabaret.

Smollett's rueful conclusion on the social *mores* of the time was that

It is pretty extraordinary that it should not be deemed a disparagement in a nobleman to sell half a pound of figs, or a palm of ribbon or tape, or to take money for a flask of sour wine: and yet be counted infamous to match his daughter in the family of a person who has distinguished himself in any one of the learned professions.[1]

The decline of the Medici bank lasts from the death of Cosimo in 1464 to the expulsion of the Medici from Florence in 1494. But, by the time of Cosimo's death, the heights of prosperity had already been passed and troubles had beset many of the branches, including that in London. Piero, who succeeded Cosimo, had received no practical training in banking. Suffering much from gout, he was largely bed-ridden during the five years when he was head of the family. He started, ill-advisedly — it is said on the devious advice of Dietisalvi Neroni — by calling in outstanding loans both at home and abroad and provoking a flood of bankruptcies. It is not, however, evident that this was the only cause of the slump. Other contributory causes were the diminishing supply of wool from England and the interruption of trade in the Levant following the outbreak of war in 1463 between Venice and the Sultan.

Lorenzo had little training and, conceivably, less interest in banking than either of his immediate predecessors and he depended too heavily on the advice of his managing director, Francesco Sassetti, until his death in 1490. Unfortunately, Sassetti was at best a guider rather than a firm leader — *capax imperii, nisi imperasset*. Machiavelli possibly summed it up when he said that Lorenzo was 'infelicissimo' in business. However that may be, two years after Lorenzo's death, at the time of the French invasion in 1494, the Medici bank was on the brink of bankruptcy.

During the whole of the fourteenth century the Medici bank had done little to promote suitable economic growth and the vast funds which it could for long command were used to finance other monarchs, or military campaigns, or to fortify alliances with the Sforza in Milan and others. None of these investments made it easy to recover the initial capital. It is, however, relevant that the Medici bank was not the only one to do badly in the last half of the fifteenth century. In 1422 there were seventy-two international banks in Florence, but by 1494 there were less than six left and it was not possible to fill all the offices in the Arte del Cambio. Florence was not to regain its paramount position as a financial capital.

Throughout the fifteenth century the Medici and their associates had shown at least sufficient business and commercial acumen to survive. They had demonstrated their skill as entrepreneurs throughout Europe whenever the occasion arose and they had used their financial power to further their own political ends. Except for accusations that Lorenzo, when latterly in financial difficulties, had misappropriated part of the bank's and public funds, no charge of financial impropriety has successfully been laid against them. To remain unscathed in this sense for 100 years entitles the Medici to an honourable place in the history of merchant banking. The Medici bank finally succumbed because of mismanagement. It is accordingly to their activities as statesmen and as patrons of the arts that we must look for their lasting fame, and it is only in the second of these that Angelo Poliziano plays a significant part. In order to see how the Medici attained their political objectives — and there are occasions when they appear as the greatest impresarios of all time — it is worth while having at least a cursory look at the Florentine system of government and the stage machinery that they were able to operate.

The Florentines had evolved a system as full of checks and counter-checks as the American Constitution. Just as those who drew up the initial ordinances across the Atlantic were determined that no single ruler, or his sycophants, should be able to manipulate the system for their own ends, so the Florentines before them, reacting against the misuse of aristocratic rule and recurring strife, were determined that no single citizen should elevate himself above his fellows. But, inevitably, the very complexities of the scheme made it liable to manipulation, particularly in the hands of the Medici.

The supreme authority in Florence was vested in the Signoria; the eight Priors elected by the Guilds, the Gonfaloniere of Justice and those of the Companies of the People united with the twelve Buonomini to form the Collegio. All of these remained during their term of office in the Palace of the Signoria; they even slept in the same room. To take important decisions affecting the lives of the citizens, a Parlamento – an assembly of all the citizens meeting in the Piazza of the Signoria – could be called, traditionally by ringing the great bell known as La Vacca. (Calling the bell by the name of the animal – the cow – round whose neck it was said to have been hung is an interesting historic example of that rare figure of speech, synecdoche.) Nothing symbolises more accurately the closely woven domestic nature of the Florentine city State than the picture of the citizens hurrying through the narrow streets from the Piazza del Duomo, past Ghiberti's gates, or across the Arno from San Miniato, to the clamour of the bell, knowing that there was some crisis in government – an attempt at rebellion perhaps, or a threatened invasion. The Parlamento retained its power, latterly in a fairly residual form, throughout the fifteenth century, but as statecraft evolved in more sophisticated hands the real significance of the ancient popular assembly diminished.

Florence was always addicted to government by committee (Balìa) and various committees or councils could be appointed for limited periods and in order to carry out allotted tasks. One committee (the Otto di Pratica), for example, was at one time in charge of foreign affairs and defence, while the highest judicial authority was the Otto di Balìa. The Florentines did, however, remain careful to limit both the authority which they delegated and the time during which it could be exercised.

There were two main features of the Florentine system which appear particularly strange in modern conditions. First, in order to ensure that there should be no possibility of a continuing dynastic rule, tenure of office was on all occasions for very short periods. The Florentines had apparently no doubt that stability and continuity were of less importance than frequent re-election. Most appointments were held for periods varying from two months to a year; as a rule office-bearers could be re-elected only after gaps of two or three years.

Secondly, there was the peculiar electoral system. From 1328 this comprised two separate stages: qualification of candidates and drawing by lot. The first scrutiny *(squittino),* which determined the eligibility of citizens for specific offices, took place every five years. The scrutinies were sub-divided; those for the Signoria and the principal offices were carried out by three eminent and respected tellers, known as the Tre Maggiori. The scrutiny for other offices, particularly administrative ones, was undertaken by the Uffici Intrinseci ed Estrinseci. But this stage did not complete the story. When a scrutiny had been completed, the names of those successful were placed in purses *(borse)* from which they would be drawn by lot when a vacancy was to be filled. The candidate whose name was drawn from the purse was appointed unless he had meanwhile become liable to some temporary disqualification. This *imborsazione,* at once the key and the most vulnerable part of the system, was carried out by the Accoppiatori for the highest offices, and by Segretari for the lesser ones. The Accoppiatori, who were sometimes granted extended tenure of office, accordingly occupied an unusually influential position. In order to get his name into the special bag *(borsellino)* from which the Gonfaloniere of Justice was chosen, the candidate had to get the votes of at least twelve of the nineteen Accoppiatori.

This was the system that the Medici operated successfully. But they were careful to act unobtrusively and, although their power increased steadily throughout the century, they held no great number of offices. Giovanni de' Bicci was elected Prior by his Guild in 1402 and was re-elected in 1406 and 1411. Cosimo was three times Gonfaloniere of Justice and served seven times as a Balìa member, but he was only once Accoppiatore for a few months from October 1440 to February 1441; and for long there was no Medici in office at all. But it seems likely that the Accoppiatori were elected with the connivance, if not the explicit consent, of the Medici. On at least two occasions, in 1459 and 1463, when the Accoppiatori had to meet to make additions to the *borse*, they met in Cosimo's palace in the Via Larga. Pope Pius II had written earlier that 'Although Cosimo is practically Signore of the town, he behaves in such a way as to appear a private citizen and prefers facts to appearances'.[2] Cosimo was also at pains to emphasise that he was only a private citizen and he sometimes found this convenient. For example, in 1463 when Pius asked him to ensure that Florence contributed to the Crusade, he replied that the Pope would know very well the limitations on the powers of any individual in a free Republic.

Vespasiano da Bisticci wrote in his *Lives* that Cosimo

knew how difficult it was to exercise political power as he had done, owing to the opposition of so many great citizens who in former times had been his equals. He acted with the greatest skill to preserve his power; and whenever he wished to achieve something, he saw to it, in order to escape envy as much as possible, that the initiative appeared to come from others and not from him.[3]

This he did even more during the last ten years of his life. Nicodemo da Pontremoli reported that, in April 1462, Cosimo had called to his house the *cittadini principali*, the names being Agnolo Acciaiuoli, Luca Pitti, Giovanni Bartoli, Luigi Ridolfi, Francesco Ventura, Otto Niccolini, Bernardo d'Alamanno de' Medici, and Tommaso Soderini. With one exception they were all Accoppiatori. This was the method by which Cosimo exerted his influence whenever the Medici interests required it.

Inevitably, in time the system began to creak. Lorenzo, with his many other intellectual and emotional preoccupations, became impatient with the minutiae of government — as of banking. On his return from his successful embassy to Naples in 1480, when he had saved Florence from imminent defeat in the war against the Pope and his allies, his personal reputation was at its highest, and a number of reforms aimed at concentrating rather than distributing power were carried out. The Signoria set up a Council of Seventy which, from then on, was the seat of power. It controlled the elections and filled vacancies by co-option. The Otto di Pratica and the Otto di Balìa became Committees of the Seventy. By the end of the 1480s there were rumours that Lorenzo intended to proclaim himself Gonfaloniere for life and, in 1490, the power of the Council of Seventy was diminished by the appointment of a Balìa of Seventeen, including Lorenzo, with power to choose the Signoria. The march towards autocracy was gathering speed.

Altogether Lorenzo's influence on elections to offices and councils was a great deal more extensive than could be justified by any of the official positions he held. Together with his associate, Ser Giovanni Guidi, he drew up the whole membership list for the scrutiny council of 1484 and, on another occasion when it came to creating the Balìa, he had nominated all the members. But he seems to have had enough of Cosimo in him to be able to tell the Milanese ambassador that he intended to proceed 'per una via indiretta'[4] and, on the whole, this is what he did.

Not until the twentieth century has another family attempted as much as the Medici in the determined use of power, specially financial power, for their own purposes. The parallel between the Kennedys and the Medici is in some respects surprisingly close. Both were strong patriarchic families and, like all those who attempt to form a dynasty, they saw their immortality in their children. Both started as financiers and used money as power. The Kennedys, like the Medici, achieved their success and their dominion over the State within an existing constitutional framework and despite the suspicion which their activities frequently aroused. The two families were much influenced by their womenfolk, and in both cases violence too frequently crossed their paths. The resemblances are remarkably symmetric and both families encouraged their own court jesters and scribes: but, in their attempt to build a new Camelot across the Atlantic and to encourage the liberal arts, the Kennedys fell far short of the achievements of the Medici. The Medici, too, enriched their city with works of art acquired from all over the world, and now lie buried in the church of San Lorenzo in tombs which mark their magnificence. On more than one occasion the Medici were driven by popular fury from their home State, a fate which has not overtaken the Kennedys.

Notes

1.   Tobias Smollett, *Travels through France and Italy* (originally published 1766, World's Classics 1907), Letter XXVII, 28 January 1765.
2.   Nicolai Rubinstein, *The Government of Florence under the Medici 1434 to 1494.*
3.   Ibid.
4.   Ibid.

2   GIOVANNI de' BICCI AND COSIMO

The Medici appear like a carefully assembled operatic cast before the backcloth of the constitutional and banking systems which they manipulated, often with seemingly inevitable success. Like good artistes, they soon dominated the stage which was set for them.

Giovanni de' Bicci was the original father figure of the Medici; the archetype who laid the foundations of the family fortunes; the cornerstone of the prosperity of the house. Not a great deal is known of his early career except that he was involved in Medici affairs in Rome, and in 1397 he moved the bank's main business to Florence. Thereafter the story, until his death in 1429, was one of steady expansion and consolidation. He was little concerned with politics or with the government of the city, but he was a Prior of his guild and, in 1421, his growing reputation was marked by his appointment as Gonfaloniere.

It is significant, or perhaps prophetic, how early he comes to notice for his interest in the arts. In 1419 he built and endowed the Foundling Hospital (Ospedale degli Innocenti) — the first recorded commission entrusted to the rising architect, Brunelleschi. He was also one of the judges in the international competition to decide on the architect to design the bronze doors of the Baptistery and he must have been a party to the selection of Ghiberti. Likewise, he must have been concerned in the decision to give Brunelleschi authority to complete the Cathedral dome. The original commission had been given to Arnolfo di Cambio in the early fourteenth century and, even then, the Signoria had said that the cathedral 'should be designed so as to be worthy of a heart expanded to much greatness, corresponding to the noble city's soul, which is composed of the souls of all its citizens.'[1] This was a prescription in keeping with Giovanni's basic philosophical attitude. Brunelleschi received other commissions from Giovanni, notably the Church of San Lorenzo which houses the tombs of the Medici family. An enlightened patronage of the arts is the recurring hallmark of the Medici from Giovanni onwards.

Giovanni's other claim to fame lies in his association with a novel tax known as the *catasto*. It is not certain that Giovanni actually invented it. The new tax was bound to bear with especial severity on his own fortune, but he realised with unusual objectivity that it was for the common good; he voted for it; and it is now generally linked with his

29

name. The object, and for once the effect, of the tax was to spread the fiscal liability more evenly. Previously the taxation imposts dated from much earlier days when Florence was mainly an agricultural community and taxes were levied on land, but movable property, which by now comprised most of the wealth of the rich merchants, escaped very lightly. The catasto was based on individual returns, called *portate*. Each head of a household had to list his property, his stock in the public Monte Comune and his business investments and was required to produce his last balance-sheet or company report in surprising detail. The portate were abridged in huge volumes, called the *campioni,* many of which are still preserved. And, finally, there was a summary, called the *sommario,* which gave the name of the taxpayer and the amount of his tax. (The form of abridgement and summary and the method of engrossing were strangely similar to the recording of property conveyances in the Scottish Register of Sasines which survives into this century.)

The catasto had the virtue — much ahead of its time — that it was based on ability to pay, and dwelling-houses, for example, were exempt. Not that the tax was popular and, with a familiar ring, the citizens denounced it for discouraging initiative, restricting business, etc. Under the law of 1427 the catasto was to be levied every three years, but this provision proved too onerous. The catasto did, however, remain workable without too many complications, in odd contrast to modern Italian fiscal law. Luigi Einaudi, the great economist, estimated not so long ago that if all the statutory taxes were enforced today they would consume more than the whole national income. The total effect of the fifteenth-century fiscal system is best exemplified by looking at the tax paid, a little later, by Cosimo according to the 1457 catasto:

Table 1   Tax Due from Cosimo de' Medici and Pierfrancesco, his Nephew, According to Their Return For The Catasto of 1457

	f.	s.	d.
Total value of real estate excluding the two palaces in via Larga, the Villas of Careggi, Cafaggiolo, and Trebbio, and the houses in Pisa and Milan	59,741	18	8
Four slaves	120	0	0
Stock in Monte Comune or in the public debt	8,569	8	0
Business investments	54,238	8	0
Total of assets (sostanze)	122,669	14	8

	f.	s.	d.	f.	s.	d.
Deductions (detrazioni):						
Five percent for administrative expense						
on value of real estate, viz. f. 59,700	2,985	0	0			
120 pairs of oxen $\frac{120 \ \times \ 100}{7}$	1,714	5	8*			
Fourteen mouths (bocche) at f. 200	2,800	0	0	7,499	5	8
Taxable wealth (sovrabbondante)				115,170	9	0

Computation of tax:			
One-half percent on sovrabbondante		575	17	1
Three heads (teste) — Piero, Giovanni, and Pierfrancesco			18	0
Amount of tax		576	15	1

*The Catasto laws allowed a deduction of one florin annual income for each pair of oxen used to cultivate farmland. Canestrini, *L'arte di stato*, p. 172.
Source: ASF, Medicco avanti il Principato, filza 82, fols. 559–597. [2]

Before we leave this interesting tax, the comparative wealth of the Medici family is also emphasised in the list of taxpayers who paid more than 50 florins, according to the 1457 catasto:

Table 2   List of the Taxpayers Who Paid More than 50 Florins According to the 1457 Catasto

		f.	s.	d.
1.	Cosimo di Giovanni and Pierfrancesco de ' Medici	576	15	1
2.	Heirs of Giovanni d'Amerigo Benci	132	10	8
3.	Giovanni di Paolo Rucellai	102	17	2
4.	Castello di Piero Quaratesi	98	12	0
5.	Tanai di Francesco Nerli	88	18	1
6.	Jacopo di Messer Andrea dei Pazzi	84	3	7
7.	Andrea di Lapo Guardi	70	11	9
8.	Gino di Neri di Gino di Neri Capponi	63	18	4
9.	Jacopo di Piero Baroncelli	60	10	9
10.	Andrea di Francesco Banchi	54	4	8
11.	Sons of Antonio di Messer Andrea dei Pazzi	51	15	10
	Total	1,384	17	11[3]

Giovanni remained a banker with a bias towards the trading aspects of his profession; high finance came later with his son, Cosimo. But he showed in full measure the prevailing Medici virtues of courtesy, a warm and generous disposition and a degree of magnanimity towards his adversaries which was quite exceptional in his century. The portrait of him by Bronzino shows a strong face, not unkindly but full of character. The Medici were seldom of a handsome appearance and most of them suffered − sometimes fatally − from gout and eczema.

It was the custom of the age that, with the full solemnity of religious office, a dying deposition should be made at some length, or at least recorded by a contemporary author. In Giovanni's case, Cavalcanti reports him as saying:

I leave you with a larger business than any other merchant in the Tuscan land, and in the enjoyment of the esteem of every good citizen and of the great mass of the populace, who have ever turned to our family as to their guiding star. If you are faithful to the traditions of your ancestors, the people will be generous in giving you honours. To achieve this, be charitable to the poor, kindly and gracious to the miserable, lending yourselves with all your might to assist them in their adversity. Never strive against the will of the people, unless they advocate a baneful project. Speak not as though giving advice, but rather discuss matters with gentle and kindly reasoning. Be chary of frequenting the Palace; rather wait to be summoned, and then be obedient, and not puffed up with pride at receiving many votes. Have a care to keep the people at peace, and to increase the commerce of the city. Avoid litigation or any attempt to influence justice, for whoso impedes justice will perish by justice.[4]

Giovanni was sixty-eight when he died. Machiavelli summed up his character in saying:

He never sought the honours of government, yet enjoyed them all. When holding high office he was courteous to all. Not a man of great eloquence, but of an extraordinary prudence.[5]

How had Giovanni managed to build so well that his heir Cosimo was, in a short space of time, able to dominate the entire state? First, Giovanni was fortunate in his timing. During his lifetime the power in Florence lay with an oligarchy of the ruling families, and it was an oligarchy based on wealth. Giovanni saw very clearly that in such a climate influence was in direct proportion to financial resources. So he pushed steadily ahead, expanding both his banking interests and the trade on which banking depended. He was originally regarded as something of an upstart but the Albizzi, under the moderate Maso, and the other influential families thought it prudent to treat with him, and the conflict between the Albizzi and the Medici did not come to a head until after Giovanni's death.

Secondly, he sought no part in political intrigues. Trade and the interests of his family were his abiding concern, and apart from a lively affection for the arts, which came easily to all the Medici, he had no other interests. His modest way of life accorded well with the austerity of his time — the trend towards more bourgeois, and then more extravagant, habits was to develop in the next two generations. He was the kind of man whom, today, any Government would be happy to make a member of a Royal Commission, but who would decline higher office.

In many ways Cosimo (1389—1464) is the most fascinating of all the Medici and the one who seemed best able to keep his inner being safe from scrutiny. Less spectacular in his way of life, less versatile and less of an extrovert than Lorenzo, he had an uncanny way of winning respect and then affection. He alone of his family was granted the unusual title of Pater Patriae, and a burial place in the interior of the Church of San Lorenzo. Cosimo brought to perfection the art of ruling without seeming to rule. In the words of Pope Pius II:

> Nothing is denied to Cosimo. He is the arbiter of peace and of war, and the moderator of the laws. Not so much a private citizen as the lord of the country. The policy of the Republic is discussed in his house; he it is who gives commands to the magistrates. Nought of royalty is wanting to him save the name and the state of a kind.[6]

Put another way, he accomplished that most difficult of tasks, he carried success into a second generation. He had to be better than the father and, as it turned out, he was.

But he was full of contradictions. For a profound scholar and the promoter of Platonic studies, it is strange that he retained a keen interest in astrology. His enthusiasm for chess was more consistent. (Later tycoons have been known to say that their favourite amusement was chess — with humans.) But he remained austere in all his habits and attitudes. When his wife, Contessina, asked him what was the subject of his meditations, he replied tersely:

When we are going to our country-house, you are busy for a fortnight preparing for the move, but since I have to go from this life to another, does it not seem to you that I ought to have something to think about?[7]

This is consistent with his macabre reply to Contessina when, shortly before his death, she asked why he closed his eyes so much. 'To accustom them to it.'

Cosimo became the greatest financier in Italy, if not in Europe. He was already forty years old when he succeeded his father and he had undergone a wide training in commercial, political and diplomatic life. He had visited branches of the family firm throughout Europe and worked regularly in the bank. He went on official missions to Milan, Bologna, Lucca and Rome. More widely travelled than his father, he was also a more adventurous trader. Throughout all his banking activities he displayed that uncanny sense of purpose which marks the aspiring millionaire. In his case God was working for the florin – the Medici florin.

Ironically, the beginning of his rule as head of the family was marked by his only major reverse. As bankers the Medici had aroused increasing envy among some of the leading Florentine families, not least the Albizzi. Rinaldo degli Albizzi came from the biggest wool and cloth merchants in Florence. He had received a wider diplomatic training than Cosimo and had proved himself in the war against Lucca. Proud, hot-headed and impulsive, he was unable to play second fiddle to Cosimo, and he began to lay his plans accordingly. *Hubris* was the charge laid against Cosimo. He was accused of setting himself above his fellow-citizens to the detriment of the State. The Albizzi also made much of Cosimo's plans for a new Medici palace as evidence of ostentation. Cosimo, perhaps feeling that now that he was head of the family he could spread his wings, had started building a new family house in what was then called the Via Larga. Brunelleschi was given the first chance to design the new building which was intended to be a model of its kind; but it is characteristic of Cosimo that he found Brunelleschi's plan too grandiose and accepted instead a more modest one by the rising young architect, Michelozzo. Donatello was also commissioned to adorn the courtyard *(cortile)* – a fortunate commission which produced the famous bronze statues of David (now in the Bargello) and of Judith slaying Holofernes (now in the Loggia de' Lanzi).

The Albizzi had gained control of the Signoria. Cosimo was arrested and locked in a small cell (8 ft x 6 ft) in the tower of the Palazzo

Vecchio, called the Barbaria. In this dreadful confinement Cosimo showed no heroic steadfastness of purpose. He feared execution or poisoning and tried to bribe his way out – a charge of faintheartedness that pursued him for the rest of his life: but, bearing in mind the summary nature of justice and injustice as demonstrated in these days, his lack of courage can be understood, if not condoned. It is the main flaw in an admirable character.

Cosimo was sentenced to exile and his family and supporters received similar punishment. But he was to return in a year's time. After Cosimo had been removed from the scene, Rinaldo made a great mistake in failing to destroy the borse which contained the names of those eligible for office. He merely added a number of his own supporters: this proved to be insufficient. Although Rinaldo had abolished election by lot, he was compelled to restore it in the next year, and the first drawing in September 1434 produced a new Signoria, under the presidency of Nicolo Donati, which was at once favourable to the return of Cosimo. The procedure followed is of interest. A Parlamento was summoned and the Balìa which was appointed decided that Cosimo and his family should be recalled. It is odd to find a committee acting with such imperative urgency.

After Cosimo's return, Rinaldo and many of his party were exiled from Florence, often with deprivation of political rights. It was not, however, a simple reversal of what had happened on Cosimo's banishment. This went very much farther. In 1433, eight Medici, two Pucci, together with Agnolo Acciaiuoli, were banished; but a year later seventy-three of the Albizzi party were banished. This difference seemed to indicate a change in political aim. In 1433 the Albizzi had hoped to consolidate an existing regime, but in 1434 Cosimo felt strong enough to take more drastic measures in order to establish a new one, although he still intended to proceed with every appearance of democratic consultation.

Cosimo's own account of his action on recall from exile is, naturally, in more self-exculpatory terms:

> They banished many citizens and set down (i.e., made Grandi or nobles) many disloyal families and did many things favourable to the city. During their rule the Balìa given to various citizens expired, the Squittini, or Scrutinies, came to an end, and the borse, or ballot-bags, remained for five years in the hands of the Accoppiatori, that is to say, the borse of the Priors, so that they could make whomsoever they would Priors and Gonfalonieres of Justice. In January my name was the first to be drawn from the borse as Gonfaloniere, and in my

time no one was banished nor was ill done to any one. I caused the sentence of death passed upon Francesco Guadagni, and upon some others whom I found in the hands of the Captain of the Balìa, to be commuted to perpetual imprisonment. Also I ordered the armed men who stood at the door of the Palace to be removed and the Palace and the Piazza to be kept as they were before the revolution, and I prolonged the league with the Signory of Venice for ten years.[8]

It is thought that it was while he was exiled at Venice that Cosimo bought the slave girl by whom he had a son who eventually became a Canon in the Cathedral at Florence. A surprising number of family slaves were brought to Florence during the fourteenth and fifteenth centuries, mainly from Theodosia in the Crimea. The girls were shipped to Genoa and Venice, and in Florence a duty was levied on every slave who entered the city. Under a law of 1366, the flight of a slave was regarded as a serious offence. Baldovinetti, in his *Ricordi*, recalls that he bought a Tartar slave from a Venetian for 35 florins; he had to pay 25 florins duty; brokerage 1 florin; and 4 florins for clothes. He sold her three years later for 36 florins. In the fifteenth century the prices began to rise and the Florentines demanded Russian or Circassian girls who were thought to be better favoured. The liberation of slaves did not begin until the end of the fifteenth century. Slavery appears to have been tacitly ignored by most Florentines, although the free labour was no doubt welcome.

Cosimo was now at the beginning of his period of real authority. He was elected Gonfaloniere for the customary short period, but from now until his death in 1464 he was effectively in charge of the State. The consecration of the newly completed cathedral of Santa Maria del Fiore under Brunelleschi's cupola — the wonder of the civilised world — in 1436 provided an appropriate ceremony to signalise Cosimo's assumption of power. Pope Eugenius IV paid a state visit to Florence to consecrate the new cathedral, and Cosimo had his rightful place in the procession of archbishops and bishops, ambassadors and members of the Signoria. All the majesty of the Church of Rome was enlisted to mark a terrestrial event.

Foreign affairs and the exercise of diplomacy occupied much of Cosimo's attention — for a good financial reason. He was determined that Florence should be spared the burden of continuous wars which led inevitably to penal taxation. He was therefore concerned to extend the city's influence and to buttress it with his financial power when this was needed. A classical case of the merchant banker who deals first in commodities, then in credit and finally, as a corollary, in power. In the diplomatic field his main achievement was to change the alliance with Venice for one with Milan. This was effected by the Treaty of Lodi in 1455 which produced peace and stability which were to last until the Papal wars consequent upon the Pazzi conspiracy in 1478.

It was due to Cosimo's persuasion and promise to defray part of the expenses that the great ecclesiastical assembly of the century, known as the Council of Florence, came to the city. The Pope arrived on 2 January 1440 and the Patriarch of Constantinople shortly afterwards. The object of this unusual ecumenical gathering was to find some basis of unity between the Greek and Roman churches against the growing prospect of Mohammedan invasion from the East. The Council's deliberations were largely ineffective, although the findings were eventually reproduced in the Canons of Trent; but there were some interesting by-products. The presence of so many Oriental dignitaries and their camp followers in the city did not pass unnoticed by the Florentine school of painters and some eastern influence was thereafter apparent in their work. The appearance of theologians and scholars also had a profound influence on contemporary Italian thought. The Florentines were introduced to ancient Greek literature, and the great Platonist, Gemistos Plethon, came to stay in Florence. His teaching deeply influenced Cosimo. After the fall of Constantinople in 1453, Florence became the centre of Greek learning. Greek scholars led by John Argyropoulous took up their residence in the city. They gave a new impetus to the study of Plato, and Greek was so frequently studied that Poliziano said that 'Athens has not been destroyed by the Barbarians but has migrated to Florence.' It was at this time that Cosimo decided to found his Platonic Academy and appointed Marsilio Ficino to be in charge of it.

This was not the full extent of Cosimo's patronage of scholars and scholarship. He also founded the Medici Library in 1444. Its greatest treasures were the original copy of the Pandects of the Emperor Justinian which was taken to Rome in 1561 but returned to Florence three hundred years later; the manuscripts of Cicero's letters and the annals of Tacitus; the tragedies of Aeschylus and Sophocles and Caesar's Commentaries.

As a bizarre interlude, the visit of Pope Pius II to Florence in 1459 was marked by a strange hunt in the Piazza of the Signoria which was enclosed for the purpose. This was an entertainment more appropriate to ancient Rome. Inside the stockade, horses, bulls, buffaloes, wild boar and a giraffe were let loose with twenty gladiators. There was also a large ball of wood so constructed that a man could stand inside it and roll about to annoy the animals, but the crowd broke into the enclosure and, in the words of Giovanni Cambe, 'the preparations had been great, and the expense large, but the pleasure given was small.'[9]

Cosimo was fortunate in his wife. About 1413 he had married Contessina, the daughter of Giovanni de' Bardi from one of the richest banking families. The Bardi had a close connection with Britain since two of their members were made Canons of Lincoln in 1343 and another Dean of Glasgow in the same year. Contessina, called after the great Countess Matilda, was not noticeably clever and played little part in public affairs. She belonged more to the days of Dante than to the growing Renaissance movement, but she was a good housewife and she is one of the first Florentine women who emerges as a person in her own right. Not that it was easy for women to be more than helpmeets in fifteenth-century Florence. Matteo Palmieri had written:

> The duty proper to a wife is heedfully to govern the house well, provide for its wants, know all that is going on there, be watchful as to all that affects it, confer with her husband, ascertain his will, and follow it in such wise that his command, opinion, and custom shall serve as her law.[10]

The extraordinary change in human attitudes which manifested itself during the span covered by the lives of the Medici with whom we are particularly concerned is endorsed by the correspondence left by their respective wives. Although they were all fairly prolific letter writers, they wrote comparatively little in their own hand and depended on professional scribes. If they did write themselves, they added to their signatures, perhaps with understandable pride, the words 'manu propria'. But whoever were the forgotten secretaries who acted as amanuenses, they have produced a remarkably detailed record of contemporary customs and the domestic influence to which the Medici family were subject.

Contessina was often exercised about the health of her son Giovanni, who was prone to eat and drink too much. When he was twenty-one, his mother was already telling him:

> Take care what you eat, especially this Lent, or the eczema will get hold of you again. I should be glad to know what you are doing, and the same about Piero, and whether you have yet been able to do any

business. Giorgio tells me you had very bad weather going there, but even if it was bad, you arrived safely, by the grace of God. May it please Him to send you back here safe and sound. I would like to know who waits on you and looks after your things, and where you sleep. Please take the trouble to write me a few lines sometimes, so that I may have frequent news of you. I will say no more. Christ guard you.

MONNA CONTESSINA DI COSIMO IN FLORENCE
To Giovanni di Cosimo de Medici in Ferrara.[11]

Contessina was always concerned when Giovanni had to visit Rome. Giovanni was not robust and Rome was notoriously unhygienic with frequent outbreaks of plague and malaria. Averardo de' Alberti, who had been sent by Cosimo as an ambassador to Rome before Giovanni, himself wrote to Giovanni on 22 March 1444, in terms very critical of the Eternal City:

The men of the present day who call themselves Romans are very different in bearing and in conduct from the ancient inhabitants. *Breviter loquendo,* they all look like cowherds. Their women are generally handsome in face; all the rest is uncommonly dirty; the reason, they tell me, is that they all cook. They seem agreeable, but one seldom sees them. Amusements there are none, save to go to these pardons (indulgences) which are perpetual, and in these days of Lent the women frequent them, as well as those who, like me, have nothing else to do.

Ex Urbe delacerata (From the ruined city) 22 March 1443–4[12]

When Giovanni went again to Rome in 1450, there was another outbreak of plague and Contessina felt that, with an aging husband and one son, Piero, whose health was far from good, her other son, Giovanni, should not be exposed to further danger. She wrote to him on 24 February 1450:

I have not written to you since you left, for there has been no need, but now I must write, for we hear that the plague is raging there, even among better-class people. I beg of you, for the love of God, and the love I bear you, to return as soon as possible, for you know how we suffer, Cosimo and I, when you are there. Your brother also is worried, and if Cosimo had known that there was plague he would never have allowed you to go. Cosimo has perpetual fever, as he had

when you left, and the doctors say it is not gout fever, and you
know he is getting on in years, so that one cannot know what may
happen from day to day. Therefore do please return as quickly as
possible, for you know how much he has to do. I will not write more
today.[13]

Contessina's lively affection for her family is seen in a letter she
wrote to her son, Piero, when he had gone to Trebbio shortly after the
birth of Lorenzo. She wrote on 6 February 1450:

I am sending you a quarter of a goat, a hare and a kid, so I will not
send you any veal. I have received your letter and trust that God will
one day grant us this grace, and I send you the capers. Giovanni was
very anxious to try to go up there today to see Lucrezia and the
children, and said that it seemed such a long time since he had seen
you. With great difficulty I prevented him and did not let him come,
so that he should not overtire himself. Tell Lucrezia that I will have
the baby's petticoat relined, and that she shall have it on Monday,
finished. Tell her also to make him suck well, and take care of all the
children. Cosimo is well; this morning his knee pained him a little
and he had a touch of the gout. But I think he will soon be well, for
it is nothing much. If you or Lucrezia need anything, let me know. I
will say no more. Christ guard you.

In Florence on 6 February 1449–50
MA CONTESSINA IN FLORENCE
To Piero di Cosimo de Medici at Trebbio[14]

Contessina's slightly parsimonious nature is apparent in another letter
to Giovanni dated 18 December 1450:

Although I told them we paid too much for the pigs, I want thee to
send us a pig or a roe for Christmas, if they are offered to thee; if we
have to buy them we will not have them. Messer Rosello writes that
he is coming to pass Christmas with me, and has sent Cosimo a fine
cloak of Polish fashion of marten and sable, a pair of gloves, and the
tooth of a fish a foot and a half long. As we have to prepare for the
festival of the Three Kings, they will make a little change from my
cloth of gold.[15]

But no one spoke ill of her, in itself a good obituary, and if the bust of
an old woman ascribed to Donatello (now in the Museo Nazionale in

Florence) is really of Contessina, it confirms the impression of basic virtue and simple kindliness.

Shortly before his death, Cosimo wrote to Marsilio Ficino in terms of eloquent classical resignation:

> Yesterday I came to the villa of Careggi, not to cultivate my fields but my soul. Come to us, Marsilio, as soon as possible. Bring with thee our Plato's book *De Summo Bono*. This, I suppose, you have already translated from the Greek language into Latin as you promised. I desire nothing so much as to know the best road to happiness. Farewell, and do not come without the Orphean lyre.[16]

Ficino's own letter to Lorenzo shows the effect which Cosimo had on his friends:

> Inasmuch as Plato only once showed me the Idea of courage, Cosimo showed it me every day. For the moment I will not mention his other qualities. Cosimo was as avaricious and careful of time as Midas of money; he spent his days parsimoniously, carefully counting every hour and avariciously saving every second; he often lamented the loss of hours. Finally, having like Solon the philosopher (even when occupied in most serious business) diligently studied philosophy, yet even till the last day when he departed from this world of shadows to go to light he devoted himself to the acquisition of knowledge. For when we had read together Plato's book dealing with the *Origin of the Universe* and the *Summum Bonum* he, as you who were present well know, soon after quitted this life as though he was really going to enjoy that happiness which he had tasted during our conversations. Farewell, and as God fashioned Cosimo according to the Idea of the World, do you continue as you have begun to fashion yourself according to the Idea of Cosimo.
>
> MARSILIO FICINO[17]

Ficino was admittedly a protégé of Cosimo's, but there would be few in Florence who did not subscribe, in varying degrees, to his sense of loss at his patron's death. Mature and experienced when he assumed the direction of the family fortunes, Cosimo relentlessly pursued a successful trading and banking policy. It is highly probable that he was moved to take an active, though usually clandestine, part in politics purely to safeguard his commercial interests. He was of unremarkable appearance and never dressed ostentatiously, usually contenting himself with the simple, long Florentine gown known as the *lucco*. Even at the height of his power he never behaved like a tyrant – as the rulers of other Italian city-states did – and he did not surround himself with an armed guard.

He manipulated the electoral system through his hand-picked Accoppiatori, to ensure that Medici supporters were in the majority, but he himself did not seek public appointments. He was Gonfaloniere for only three periods – a total of six months' public office during a rule that lasted for thirty years. Apart from operating at one or more removes in politics he was also skilful at bringing about the financial ruin of anyone who opposed him. But his real source of power came from the aim which he shared with those he governed – peace and the growing prosperity of the city. As long as the Medici remained identified with this, and they were always popular with the lower ranks of society, they were safe.

Cosimo rejoiced in his family. He refused to make a will, saying that he trusted his children's affection. His own preoccupations were essentially serious and he disliked entertainment. He was not an artist but much more than a mere patron. He was a man of profound intellectual judgement, and the foundation of the Platonic Academy was one of the projects dearest to his heart. In the final resort, however, there is something unattractive about him, something cold and callous. The aphorisms attributed to Cosimo all tend towards the cynical, for example 'two yards of red cloth suffice to create an honourable citizen.' There is no difficulty in distinguishing him from his more modest, and more engaging father, or from his more dynamic grandson. Today the Government would be glad to call on his services to carry out some unpopular task, which he would do successfully and impassively.

Notes

1. G.F. Young, CB, *The Medici* (John Murray, London, 1910).
2. Raymond de Roover, *The Rise and Decline of the Medici Bank, 1397–1494*.
3. Ibid.
4. Janet Rose, *Lives of the Early Medici as told in Their Correspondence* (Chatto and Windus, London, 1910).
5. Young, *The Medici*.
6. Ross, *The Early Medici*.
7. Yvonne Maguire, *The Women of the Medici* (George Routledge and Sons Ltd, London, 1927).
8. Ross, *The Early Medici*.
9. Ibid.

10. Maguire, *The Women of the Medici.*
11. Ibid.
12. Ibid.
13. Ibid.
14. Ibid.
15. Ross, *The Early Medici.*
16. Ibid.
17. Ibid.

3 PIERO AND LORENZO'S SUCCESSION

The role of Piero, who succeeded Cosimo, is best seen as an intermission between the more spectacular activities of his father and his son, Lorenzo. The Medici were marking time. A younger son, Piero, came to power because of the earlier death of his brother, Giovanni. He hated violence and all forms of ostentation, and it is difficult to believe that he expected office or enjoyed it. He suffered badly from gout and is remembered for this by his sobriquet 'Il Gottoso'.

Piero made a bad start. As a banker he committed the grievous error of calling in large numbers of outstanding loans without very much in the way of notice. While this impetuous action improved the liquidity of the Medici bank, it did nothing for Piero's popularity, and he was soon faced with a conspiracy by the envious Pitti family. Luca Pitti was intent on overthrowing the Medici and he served notice to this effect by challenging a proposed loan to Galeazzo Sforza of Milan, an essential part of Piero's foreign policy. This was followed by a singularly inefficient attempt to ambush Piero on a journey between his villa at Careggi and Florence. The would-be assassins behaved with all the lack of circumspection that distinguishes the numerous band of murderers which Verdi, in his Macbeth, found necessary to dispose of Banquo. The Pitti conspirators were easily identified by Lorenzo and the ambush was forestalled. Piero was then able to suppress incipient rebellion by means of a show of force, using Milanese troops who happened to be stationed in Florence. There was no bloodshed and Piero once again exemplified the family's reputation for clemency. Even Luca Pitti himself was pardoned — to suffer the inevitable fate of a conspirator who has failed and been forgiven: he lived the rest of his life in obscure neglect. Those who had made him gifts and contributions towards the building of his great palace in the hope of favours to come, now demanded them back and claimed that they were loans. Even the workmen stopped work and left the building, which remained incomplete until it was taken over by the later Medici Grand Dukes.

The apparently inevitable way in which three Medici in succession — Cosimo, Piero and Lorenzo — each had to face one rebellion while in power, presents an oddly symmetrical pattern. It was as though each one had to survive an ordeal and then be left in peace. It also seems probable that, while the Florentines recognised the benefits which flowed from the Medici family's exercise of authority, they were not prepared to let them have it all their own way. There came a time when another family — the Albizzi, the Pitti or the Pazzi — felt strong enough to challenge the Medici. But the Medici had established a close working relationship with the gods of ancient classical mythology and on each occasion survived with their stature and reputation greatly enhanced.

Piero's foreign policy was also beset with troubles. Cosimo's main ally, Francesco Sforza, died in 1466, and the linchpin of the network of alliances was removed. But in this field Piero was more successful. He won the confidence of Louis XI of France to such an extent that the Medici were given permission to use the Lily of France in their arms:

Louis, by the grace of God King of France. We make known to all present and for the future: Bearing in mind the great, praiseworthy, and much to be commended fame enjoyed by the late Cosimo de' Medici during his life in all his actions and his affairs, which he conducted with such great virtue and prudence that his children and other relatives and friends must be commended and held in high honour. For these reasons and moved by the supplication and prayer which has been addressed to us by our friends, and by our loyal Councillor Piero de' Medici, son of the said late Cosimo de' Medici, we by our own will, special grace, full power and royal authority decree and command by those presents that the said Piero de' Medici . . . his heirs and successors born and to be born in legal wedlock may henceforward and for ever have and bear in the arms three Fleur de lis of the shape and manner herein portrayed.[1]

Thereafter one of the five Medici roundels always had a fleur-de-lis embossed on it.

Piero drew much support from his wife, Lucrezia Tornabuoni, an outstanding figure in Florentine history. Like Cosimo's wife, Contessina, she came from an old Florentine family and, although she too was diligent in her household economy, she had much wider interests. She took an active part in the politics of the time and could hold her own both with Piero and Lorenzo and their friends. A poetess in her own accord, she wrote religious songs and miracle plays in both *ottava* and *terza rima*. She was a natural poetess, and even though her poems lacked any great power, the taste and scholarship evident in her

writing prove how quick had been the advance from feudal restrictions. One of her early letters to Piero showed a more philosophical
disposition than that of Contessina. In February 1457, when she was
at Cafaggiuolo with her children, she wrote:

> I have today received a letter from you, which was very dear to me,
> since it told me how you were. I see that by the grace of God, the
> ride did not trouble you much, which pleases me. Mona Contessina
> had already told me this, and also that you were greeted with great
> rejoicings, and truly, as you say, we have much to thank God for.
> So make up your mind to suffer a little discomfort gladly, for these
> things cannot be done without weariness.[2]

In 1467 she went to Rome to start negotiations for the marriage of
Lorenzo and she made such an impression on Roman society that
Filippo Martelli wrote to Lorenzo describing her visit, during which
she had also sought certain privileges from the Pope:

> Her visit has been most valuable, for she has not only fulfilled her
> vow, but she has acquired high favour with all this Court, and
> especially with these gentlemen, in such a way that even if she had
> no more than her presence, her conversation and her appearance, it
> would show that she was greater than her reputation. I know that
> the Cardinals have talked about her, and have decided that no
> finer lady ever came to Rome. God leave you the desired comfort
> that you have in her and she in you and yours.[3]

Lucrezia suffered much from rheumatic gout and paid many visits
to the baths for treatment — still a traditional prescription in Italy.
In 1477 she bought the baths at Bagno a Morba just south of Volterra
and, with characteristic energy, set about modernising and refurbishing
them.

Lucrezia's affection for the Morba baths recalls the unexpected
addiction of the fifteenth-century Italians to bathing. Cold, hot, steam
and mineral baths were all popular, particularly those which came from
sulphur springs. Many of the Italian monasteries were sited on locations
adjacent to hot springs. There are still mineral spas in Tuscany, much
esteemed for their beneficial effect on the liver. But do their clients
remember Lucrezia, the most famous patron of Morba?

I am sending you sixteen flasks of remarkably good Greek wine, eight flasks of Poggibonsi marked in ink, and eight flasks from Colle. To us they all seem good. You had better choose. I also send you four plain puddings. I thought it well to do this, as on the arrival of the lady you might need them, and although I am sure you will have provided sufficiently, since I had this, and it seemed good to me, I thought you would like me to send it to you. The carrier has to return here, so do not send him back empty. Oranges, biscuits, and fish would be greeted with standards flying. No more. I am well, and hoping much from the Baths, by the grace of God, who I pray will preserve you. In haste on 23 May 1477.

LUCREZIA DE MEDICI at Bagno a Morba
To the Magnificent Gentleman Lorenzo de Medici in Pisa[4]

The remainder of Piero's brief rule was peaceful and a time of many festivities, including the first of the celebrated jousts (*giostre*). The citizens were beginning to anticipate the springtime which pervaded the first years after Lorenzo's accession. The joust called after Lorenzo took place on 7 February 1468 when he was twenty and his brother Giuliano, fifteen. Giuliano's joust took place some time later in 1475. They were celebrated in elegant poems by Pulci and Poliziano and in the paintings of Botticelli, described in Chapters 7 and 9.

Lorenzo's joust was designed in honour of Lucrezia Donati — although negotiations for his marriage to Clarice, from the noble Roman family of Orsini, had already started. As early as 1465 Lorenzo had been enamoured of the beautiful Lucrezia, the wife of Pietro Ardinghelli, a wealthy eastern merchant who was conveniently despatched to the Levant soon after his marriage, leaving the way clear for Lorenzo. It was for Lucrezia that he had organised the spectacular ball in the Papal rooms at Santa Maria Novella, a scene which he described in his *Selve d'Amore*.

The jousts provided for the Florentines a combination of all social and athletic graces although the tournaments themselves were utterly harmless. Something of their colour, excitement and pageantry can still be seen in the skilful banner-waving at the Palio, the horse-race round the Piazza in Siena. The knights arrived with their own standards and their pages. Lorenzo's entry, heralded by trumpeters, was preceded by a page bearing his banner of purple and white with a sun and a rainbow, together with his motto 'Le Temps Revient' and a laurel wreath. He was followed by twelve leading young Florentines, and then his brother, Giuliano. In the middle of Lorenzo's shield was the great Medici diamond 'Il Libro', valued at over 2,000 ducats. He rode a grey horse lent to him for the day by King Ferrante. His armour was made by the famous armourer of Milan and lent to him by the Duke. For the tournament itself he rode a charger which had been sent by Borso d'Este and, after breaking a few lances, he was awarded the first prize.

In his Ricordi, Lorenzo describes the tournament in notably cool terms:

> To do as others had done I held a joust in the Piazza Santa Croce at great expense and with great pomp. I find we spent about 10,000 ducats *di suggello*, and although I was not highly versed in the use of weapons and the delivery of blows, the first prize was given to me; a helmet fashioned of silver, with Mars as the crest.[5]

He showed even less excitement in describing his marriage to Clarice:

> I took Donna Clarice, daughter of Jacopo Orsini, to wife, or rather, she was given to me in December 1468, and the marriage was celebrated in our house on the 4th June 1469.[6]

Lorenzo refused to visit Rome to see his bride-to-be, but Clarice brought a handsome dowry described by the Archbishop of Pisa:

> Everything has been agreed to in the following fashion, *videlicet*: That they give a dower of 6,000 Roman florins in money, jewels, and dresses; which they stipulate should return to their heirs should she not have children or dispose of it by will. They agree that you should not give her the fourth part of the dower, as is customary here; and in this and all other matters, the Florentine usage and custom is to be followed save in the restitution of the dower if she dies *sine filiis et intestata*.[7]

The marriage was not a success. The choice of Clarice was one of the few mistakes made by Lorenzo's mother, Lucrezia. It was she who went to Rome to inspect her prospective daughter-in-law and she reported to her husband, with seeming objectivity:

> On Thursday morning, going to St Peter's, I met Madonna Maddalena Orsini, the sister of the Cardinal, with her daughter, who is aged fifteen or sixteen. She was dressed in the Roman fashion with a cloak, and clad thus she seemed to me very beautiful, big and fair,

but as the girl was covered I could not see her to my satisfaction. It so happened that yesterday I went to see the said Monsignor Orsini, in his sister's house, which is next to his own. After I had greeted him suitably on your behalf, his sister came in with the girl, who was dressed in a tight Roman dress, without a cloak. We stayed talking a long time, and I looked carefully at the girl. As I said, she is fairly big, and fair, and has nice manners, though she is not as sweet as our girls. She is very modest and will soon learn our customs. Her hair is not fair, for there is none such here, but it is reddish and she had plenty of it. Her face is rather round, but it does not displease me. Her throat is graceful, but a little thin, or rather delicate. We could not see her bosom, as it is the custom here to wear it entirely covered, but it seems good. She does not carry her head erect, like our girls, but holds it a little forward which I think is due to shyness. Her hand is long and graceful. Altogether we consider that the girl is quite out of the common, but she is not to be compared with Maria, Lucrezia and Bianca. Lorenzo himself has seen her, and you can hear how he liked her. I think that whatever you and he are agreed upon will be right, and I will give my consent. Let us leave it to God to guide us aright.[8]

Clarice's background was orthodox, almost feudal, and although she was not illiterate, she had neither the taste, wit nor intelligence of Lucrezia, and her relationship with her husband was never a close one. It has been said that Lorenzo would have done better to choose a Florentine bride rather than to marry one who came from Rome and from a family noted for its arrogance and pride, defects which were transmitted to her son. But this is perhaps an unnecessarily severe judgement.

On the death of Piero in the same year as Lorenzo's marriage, 700 citizens met in the Church of Sant' Antonio. The meeting was not a Pratica, an official meeting summoned by the Signoria, but a gathering of Medici supporters. The proceedings were started by Tommaso Soderini who had been a loyal supporter of Piero, and the meeting unanimously agreed that the Medici brothers, Lorenzo and Giuliano, should be preserved '*in reputatione e grandeza*'. This may seem a vague decision but it reflects very clearly the kind of authority and ascendency which the Medici enjoyed. Lorenzo had to accept when the following day, the *Principali della citta e dello stato* asked him to assume the care of both, although he states that he did so unwillingly:

The second day after his death, although I, Lorenzo, was very young, being twenty years of age, the principal men of the city and of the State came to us in our house to condole with us on our loss and to encourage me to take charge of the city and of the State, as my grandfather and my father had done. This I did, though on account of my youth and the great responsibility and perils arising therefrom, with great reluctance, solely for the safety of our friends and of our possessions. *For it is ill living in Florence for the rich unless they rule the State.* Till now we have succeeded with honour and renown, which I attribute not to prudence but to the grace of God and the good conduct of my predecessors.[9]

The pinnacle of the Medici fortunes was reached in the person of Lorenzo. Born in 1449, he was aged twenty when he succeeded his father, and he ruled till his death in 1492. Marsilio Ficino, who had taught him Platonic philosophy, said that Lorenzo had the three graces of splendour, lightheartedness and rejuvenescence. Unlike his father, Lorenzo had been brought up as the heir apparent. His tutor had been the distinguished scholar, Gentile Becchi of Urbino; he had been taught Italian literature by Landino; and his Greek teacher had been Argyropoulous. No one could have had more erudite professors. The real quality which makes Lorenzo the prime representative of the Renaissance is his versatility. He held his own as an art patron; he was passionately interested in architecture, especially if it displayed some antique influence; one of his favourite books was Alberti's *Treatise on Architecture*. Poets and artists thought of him as one of themselves and his real friends were all men of letters. He was an elegant poet in his own right and did much to restore the reputation of the native tongue as a civilised language. Physically he was strong but, like all the Medici, scarcely handsome.

Lorenzo's rule can be seen in three clear phases. First, there is the time symbolised by the springtime motto 'Le Temps Revient'; next, there are the troubled years — the Pazzi conspiracy and the war with Pope Sixtus; then there is the long period until his death when his rule and authority were consolidated. There is a difference between his rule and that of Cosimo. The patriarch Cosimo manipulated the power in the State so as to conduct affairs as he wanted. Lorenzo was able to go much farther and his authority can appropriately be described as rule. It was apparent, not only to him but to many Florentine families, that a simplistic republic was too prone to be torn by domestic feuds and that an unobtrusive autocracy was needed. Within the democratic framework, and yet without any standing military support, he was able to exercise complete authority. A strange feature is that, despite the unlimited power which he eventually exercised, he was never accused of arrogance, a vice much detested in the Albizzi, the Pazzi and other leading Florentine families. The first nine years of Lorenzo's rule were marked by great festivity and amusements as was appropriate to the youthful *brio* of Lorenzo and Giuliano. Lorenzo's circle of wits and poets vied with each other in the *divertissements* which they provided. This was the time of masques, plays and banquets where topical verse, often of a highly licentious nature, was read by the author. There were musical evenings outside Florence at the villa at Careggi and poems in Latin and the native Tuscan tongue (keenly advocated by Lorenzo) had their place there too.

Lorenzo set the temper of the time. His own poems, whether they were *ballate, canzoni di ballo* or *canzoni carnascialesche*, have survived as much more than period pieces. But pageantry as such seems to have struck a particular chord in Lorenzo. Showmanship is never far below the Italian surface and Luigi Barzini in *The Italians* pointed out that the one characteristic which is common to the most prominent Italian figures — Cola di Rienzo, Casanova and Mussolini are good examples — was their ability to see themselves in heightened terms against their own background. It was so too with Lorenzo. He reorganised the masquerades when the streets were filled with *trionfi*, carriages decorated in allegorical or mythical fashion, *carri* manned by the trade guilds, and masked riders. Lorenzo's own contribution was to replace the now hackneyed songs with new airs and metres of a kind he found more congenial. According to Grazzini:

> The first of these masquerades was performed by men who sold sugar-plums and *berriquocoli* (small cakes), and the music, for three voices, was written by a certain Arrigo Tedesco, head of the choir of San Giovanni, a musician of great repute in those days.[10]

Youth was at the prow and pleasure at the helm. There were midnight tournaments and fireworks. Filippo Corsini's account of the snowballing at the house of the beautiful Marietta Palla Strozzi is symptomatic. He describes with great zest the torches, the trumpets, the flutes, the voices of the crowd in the flickering light, the occasional marksmanship of the snowballers and the excitement and exhilaration of Marietta herself.

Lorenzo always enjoyed the company of women — except his poor wife, Clarice — but his love affairs were no more outrageous than the times allowed. In fact, he seems to have been remarkably constant. Lucrezia Donati was his first love and for long held his whole attention. Towards the end of his life, his last *affaire* was with Bartolomea de' Nasi who was said to be witty and attractive though not beautiful. And he had a long-standing friendship with Ippolita Maria Sforza, daughter of the Duke of Milan, which dated from the time when he went as a young man to represent Florence at her marriage with Don Alfonso of Aragon, Duke of Calabria, the second son of the King of Naples. She was of help to him during his embassy to Naples in 1479; she continued to write to him for some years after and the sophisticated nature of their relationship — here she is sending Lorenzo gloves for another of his girl-friends — is seen in her last letter to him which has survived, dated December 1486:

I cannot tell you the pleasure it gave me to see your handwriting and I have found even more pleasure in seeing your nephew, as I think he has something of you about him; and God knows how I long to see you, so that I can thank you with my own lips for all you have done for me and mine; for I am sure that I could not be more obliged to anyone than to Your Lordship, though you have been acting for yourself since you know that our affairs are your affairs. Magnifico Lorenzo mio, I do not know how your wife would like your taking so much care of the soul you wot of, for those who indulge in such devotions observe vigils not written in the calendar. However, to obey you, though without sharing the wickedness, I send you the gloves and some other trifles suited to your devotion. If you want anything else, say so, for I am as glad to do anything to please you as I should be for my own brothers.[11]

But Simonetta Vespucci was the Florentine who taught the torches to burn bright. The most admired of all the beauties of Florence, it is not, however, certain that she was ever Lorenzo's mistress. Born in Genoa, from a family called dei Cattanei, she had married Marco Vespucci, a prominent Florentine citizen, at the age of sixteen. Her gentle manner was such that her surpassing beauty aroused no envy. All men loved her and no woman hated her. Her moment of triumph came at Giuliano's joust in the Piazza Santa Croce in 1475 when she was the tournament Queen of Beauty. It was then apparent that Giuliano, carrying Verrocchio's helmet and standard, was first in her favour. But Poliziano, in his poem on the joust, and Botticelli in his paintings of her in the Primavera and the Birth of Venus, both reproduced emotion that goes far beyond a distant or disembodied affection. But then, when even so winning a person might have had difficulty in ordering her affairs, Simonetta executed the perfect operatic solution — she died, mourned by the whole of Florence, and by future librettists deprived of what could have been the most dramatic of all plots.

She died in April 1476 and she was carried to the church of Ognissanti on an open bier. Like another much later beauty who was also the subject of a famous painting, Gainsborough's Mrs Moncrieff, she died of what was then called consumption. Allowing for differences in fashion, the same incandescent beauty shines in both their faces, and both died young.

The Medici spring was over. Simonetta's death was followed a few months later by the murder of Galeazzo Sforza, Duke of Milan: the delicate balance of power among the Italian city States was upset, and Lorenzo was soon attacked at home and abroad. Though he survived both onslaughts, things were never the same again. The youthful abandon could not be recaptured. Scholarly, worldly, humanist, the spirit of these years shows in Lorenzo's own haunting lines:

> Quant 'è bella giovenezza
> Che si fugge tuttavia;
> Chi vuol'esser lieto, sia;
> Di doman non c'è certezza.

What's to come is still unsure. It is as though Lorenzo realised that the hedonistic life of his early years could become overripe like the mulberry. The hot Tuscan sun brings everything quickly to fruition. The high tide had turned too soon. Ronsard had the same reflection in the next century:

> Donc, si vous me croyez, mignonne,
> Tandis que vostre âge fleuronne
> En sa plus verte nouveauté,
> Cueillez, cueillez vostre jeunesse:
> Comme à ceste fleur la vieillesse
> Fera fernir vostre beauté.

Meanwhile a more sinister time lay ahead, and the avenging fury of Savonarola was still to come.

Notes

1.   Janet Ross, *Lives of the Early Medici as told in Their Correspondence* (Chatto and Windus, London, 1910).
2.   Yvonne Maguire, *The Women of the Medici* (George Routledge and Sons Ltd, London, 1927).
3.   Ibid.
4.   Ibid.
5.   Ross, *The Early Medici*.
6.   Selwyn Brinton, *The Golden Age of the Medici* (Methuen, London, 1925).
7.   Ross, *The Early Medici*
8.   Maguire, *The Women of the Medici*.
9.   Ross, *The Early Medici*.
10.   Ibid.
11.   L. Collinson-Morley, *The Early Medici* (George Routledge and Sons Ltd, London, 1935).

4 THE RULE OF THE MAGNIFICENT

Like many Renaissance princes, Lorenzo was passionately fond of horses. He was perpetually adding to his stud which he kept at Poggio a Caiano and he sent emissaries as far as the Barbary coast and Egypt to buy stallions and mares. The Neapolitan breed was also famous and Lorenzo had many dealings with King Ferrante of Naples from whom he once bought twenty mares at a time. The names of two of his favourite mounts have survived — Morello, so called for its colour, which was amenable only to his discipline, and Dormio, which he was keen to enter for the Palio.

Lorenzo was soon to need all his nerve as a rider when faced with the conspiracy of the Pazzi and their allies in Rome. In many respects the Pazzi family were the inevitable opponents of the Medici. Their origins, interests and careers were altogether too similar. The two families were for long on friendly terms. Cosimo had magnanimously allowed the Pazzi to re-enrol among the people in order to recover their political rights and he had employed one of the family, Andrea, as ambassador on several missions. Andrea had also been one of the five Accoppiatori on whom Piero depended for much of his rule. Piero had even married his daughter, Bianca, to Guglielmo Pazzi, hoping to end the rivalries between the families. Like the Medici, too, the Pazzi patronised the arts, sometimes with outstanding success, as when they commissioned Brunelleschi to design their chapel in the cloisters of Santa Croce.

The member of the family to start the rebellion proved to be Franceschino de' Pazzi. Small of stature, hot-tempered, full of vanity, greatly affected in his dress, he was a splendid example of the rich, dandified son of a noble house who lacks the integrity and the *gravitas* to make the most of his opportunities. He suffered from the mistaken belief that with charm, education and social position he could buy anything, even influence and friends, and he was only too ready to make common cause against the Medici.

Common cause was not hard to find in the ambitious scheming of Pope Sixtus IV. Originally Francesco della Rovere, Sixtus had a good record until he was appointed to the Holy See, but eventually he became obsessed with founding a dynasty and particularly with advancing the cause of his two nephews, Piero and Girolamo Riario, who were not the most attractive characters in Papal history. The Pope's plans were, however, continually frustrated by the Medici. His acquisition of Imola in the Emilian Plain as a means of pushing forward the Papal frontiers had annoyed the Florentines and when, in a further sortie, he threatened Borgo San Sepolcro, which was coming sinisterly near to the Medici domain, Florence sent a protective force of 6,000 men. The Medici had also taken great pains to oppose the elevation of Francesco Salviati to be Archbishop of Pisa. In short, the Medici had in a fairly short space of time incurred the frustrated hatred of the Archbishop, the continued fury of the Pope and the jealousy of the Pazzi.

Girolamo Riario seems to have made the first approach to involve the Pazzi family in the conspiracy. They then enlisted Montesecco, a Captain in the Pope's service, to be the principal assassin, and the records of their conversation show clearly that, although he ingenuously affected innocence, the Pope himself knew of the plot. The next move was for the young Cardinal Riario to ask Lorenzo if he could visit the Medici Palace to inspect the treasures and he proposed a Sunday visit when he could also join the Medici family in celebrating High Mass at the Cathedral. The plan was admirably simple. It was to execute the murder in the church. But Montesecco, when he learned the details, would have no part in this sacrilege and two accomplice priests, Maffei of Volterra and Stefano da Bagnone, took his place. They made a botch of the job. As befitted a generous host, Lorenzo accompanied the young Cardinal from the Medici Palace to the Cathedral. The conspirators were alarmed that Giuliano was not there and Pazzi and Bernardo Bandini went to fetch him. As the very epitome of hypocrisy, and prudence, Pazzi threw his arm round Giuliano, apparently in friendship but in reality to confirm that he was not wearing a shirt of mail, and soon they were all in the church — murderers and victims alike.

With a nice sense of drama, the Pazzi had chosen the signal for the murder as the elevation of the host. At the very moment when heads were bowed and the congregation had reached their moment of serenity, Bandini stabbed Giuliano; Francesco de' Pazzi followed with a further fierce thrust; and Giuliano was killed. Otherwise the conspirators were less lucky. Maffei only succeeded in striking Lorenzo's neck. Lorenzo threw his mantle over his left arm and, using it to parry further blows, escaped to the Sacristy where the faithful Poliziano barred the brass doors. Antonio Rodolfo sucked the wound in Lorenzo's neck lest it be poisoned and eventually Lorenzo was escorted by a detour to his own Palace. His friends took care that he should not see his brother's body lest he should be overcome with grief.

Meanwhile, Archbishop Salviati, with a gang of armed followers, went to the Palace of the Signoria and attempted to seize control. But they aroused the suspicion of the perceptive Gonfaloniere, Cesare Petrucci, who raised the alarm and seized the Archbishop and his followers. Petrucci ordered the great bell to be sounded for a Parlamento. But, while the Pazzi supporters hurried on horseback towards the Piazza dei Signori shouting aloud the ancient watchword 'Popolo e Liberta', the Medici supporters were sufficiently aroused by their counter-cry of 'Vivano le Palle'. Events moved quickly to their climax. The early conspirators were hurled alive from the windows of the Palace of the Signoria into the Piazza. The same evening, although Cardinal di Riario was saved with difficulty, Jacopo di Poggio, Archbishop Salviati and Franceschino de' Pazzi were all hanged from the windows of the Palace. None of the conspirators escaped. Bernardo Bandini fled to Constantinople from whence the Sultan eventually returned him in chains to Florence. In the three days from 26 to 28 April more than seventy men were hanged. The Medici adherents raged through the streets shouting 'Palle, Palle, down with the traitors.' The wretched Montesecco escaped capture for some days but was eventually caught and executed in the Palazzo del Podesta. Before he died he signed a confession which confirmed the complicity of Pope Sixtus in the plot. The name of the Pazzi was excised from Florentine records. They suffered the inevitable fate of conspirators who fail. History has no mercy on would-be assassins whose plans are too complicated or are simply unsuccessful. The people were indignant at the Pazzi family, not only for their attempt on the lives of the Medici brothers, but for their daring to seize the State almost incidentally. Lorenzo, with unusual compassion, saved not only Girolamo Riario but also Raffaelo Maffei, the brother of the priest who had tried to murder him, and Averardo Salviati, a relation of the Archbishop. But Giuliano was gone. Giuliano, always popular with the Florentines, had been a great athlete and jouster and at the same time a convinced patron of the arts and a versifier in his own right. He is buried in the Old Sacristy in San Lorenzo.

The Pope was not amused at the failure of the Pazzi, but it was difficult to see how the Medici could now be unseated in their own city. The Pope accordingly deployed his ultimate sanction. He published a Bull excommunicating Florence. Lorenzo's ironic reply showed that he appreciated the humour of the situation when he said that he and his people were to be excommunicated since he himself had failed to be assassinated.

The Signoria in a later letter to the Pope were firmly behind Lorenzo. 'We and our people with one voice acclaim him the defender of our liberties.' War now spread throughout central Italy and the Pope was able to muster against Florence the forces of Naples, Siena, Lucca and Urbino. Lorenzo could count only on the friendly sympathy of the French King Louis XI and, in the spasmodic fighting which followed, Florence had marginally the worst of it. Artillery was used on both sides and in the Duke of Urbino's army there were five field pieces called bombards with the remarkable names of The Cruel, The Desperate, The Victory, Ruin and None of your Jaw. Buffaloes were used to drag the bombards into place and there was much determined but inconclusive fighting over such places as the fortified town of Colle and Poggio Imperiale.

The balance of advantage was gradually turning against Florence when Ludovico Sforza, who now had the real power in Milan, helped Lorenzo to make an approach to the King of Naples — whose support for the Pope was the strength of the Papal alliance. Lorenzo decided on a course of the utmost hazard, nothing less than placing himself in the hands of the King of Naples and seeking his friendship.

There is no more dramatic event in the whole of the Renaissance, or for that matter in subsequent European, history. Lorenzo knew that he was taking a calculated risk; and he realised that the odds were scarcely in his favour. Some thought he had taken an irresponsible gambler's chance. In Guicciardini's view his going to Naples was 'too bold and rash a decision, for he put himself in the hands of a King by nature treacherous, unstable and bitterly opposed to him.'[1] A perilous attempt it certainly was, but Lorenzo was able to produce a fair argument in justification:

To the Signoria of Florence,
from Lorenzo de' Medici
Most Illustrious My Lords — It is not from presumption that I did not notify the reason of my departure to Your Illustrious Excellencies, but because it seemed to me that the agitated and disturbed condition of our city demands acts and not words. I conceive that she desires, and indeed has extreme need of peace. Seeing that all other endeavours have been fruitless, I have determined to run some peril in my own person rather than expose the city to disaster. Therefore, with the permission of Your Excellencies of the Signoria,

I have decided to go openly to Naples. Being the one most hated and persecuted by our enemies I may by placing myself in their hands be the means of restoring peace to our city. One of two things is certain, either His Majesty the King loves our city as he has asserted and some have believed, and is attempting to gain our friendship by affronting us rather than by despoiling us of liberty; or His Majesty really desires the ruin of this Republic. If his intentions are good there is no better way of testing them than by placing myself voluntarily in his power, and I make bold to say that this is the only way to make peace and to render the condition of our city stable. If His Majesty the King intends to attack our liberty it seems to me well to know the worst quickly, and that one should be injured rather than the many. I am most glad to be that one, for two reasons: first, because being the principal object of our enemies' hatred I can more easily and better explain all to the King, as it may be that our enemies only seek to injure me. The other reason is that having a greater position and larger stake in our city, not only than I deserve but probably than any citizen in our days, I am more bound than any other man to give up all to my country, even my life. These are the feelings with which I go, for perchance our Lord God desires that this war, which began with the blood of my brother and my own, should be put an end to by me. My ardent wish is that either my life or my death, my misfortunes or my well-being, should contribute to the good of our city. I shall therefore carry out my idea. If it succeeds according to my wishes and hopes I shall be most glad to benefit my country at the risk of my life and at the same time to save myself. Should evil befall me I shall not complain if it benefits our city, as it certainly must; for if our adversaries only aim at me, they will have me in their hands; if they want aught else it will be patent to all. I am certain that our citizens will unite to protect their liberty, so that by the grace of God it will be defended as was always done by our fathers. I go full of hope, and with no other object than the good of the city, and I pray God to give me grace to perform what is the duty of every man towards his country. I commend myself humbly to Your Excellencies of the Signoria.
    – From San Miniato on the 7th day of December 1479.

Your Excellencies' Servant,
LAURENTIUS DE MEDICIS[2]

The Signoria approved his decision and regularised his status by appointing him as their ambassador to the Court of Naples with plenipotentiary powers. Lorenzo's embassy was eventually successful. There is no clear record of what arguments he used, but at least one extraneous event came to his assistance. Otranto, in the south-east of the Italian peninsula, was captured by the Turks. The sinister implications of the new threat were immediately apparent both to the King of Naples, who recalled his son, the Duke of Calabria, from Siena, and to the Pope, who cancelled his interdict against Florence. Peace was restored and the Treaty eventually prepared required Florence to ask the Pope's pardon for her offences (sic); the places taken from the Florentines during the war were to be restored; the survivors of the Pazzi family to be freed from their incarceration in Volterra; and an alliance to be solemnised between Naples and Florence. Lorenzo returned in triumph and Poliziano described the occasion in appropriate Latin verse:

> Maxima sed densum capiunt vix atria vulgus;
> Toto salutantum vocibus aula fremit,
> . . . Cunctis celsior ipse patet.

Machiavelli comments that Lorenzo had 'recovered in peace all that adverse fortune had taken from him in war.' His position in Florence was not again to be seriously challenged.

Botticelli was another who celebrated Lorenzo's return in the allegorical form of his painting of Pallas subduing the Centaur. The beastly Centaur, symbol of the Pazzi conspiracy, is seen cowering before the Goddess of Wisdom bearing Lorenzo's private crest.

If this was the climax of his power and influence, the remaining twelve years of his rule (1480–92) were little disturbed by wars or upheavals. Admittedly there were two minor assassination attempts – if attempts on one's life can ever be called minor. In 1481 Battista Frescobaldi and two accomplices tried to stab him in the Church of the Carmali; but this met with no more success than a later plot conceived by Girolamo Riario. Lorenzo's last war also started in 1481 when he decided to side with the Duke of Ferrara who was threatened by Venice with the help of the Papal states. The war lasted until the Peace of Bagnolo brought it to an end in 1484. Ironically the two rival commanders – the Duke of Urbino in charge of the Florentine and allied troops, and Roberto Malatesta of Rimini who led the Venetian forces (who were both killed in battle) were such lifelong friends that they had entrusted responsibility for their children and estates to each other in the event of their death. After the end of the Ferrarese hostilities, Lorenzo consolidated a triple alliance with Naples and Milan to hold

the balance against the combined influence of Venice and the Papacy —
a balance that lasted until his death.

Not unnaturally, Lorenzo was increasingly concerned about his heirs.
He was reported as saying that he had three sons; one good (Giuliano);
one wise (Giovanni); and one a fool (Piero). According to Guicciardini,
Lorenzo feared that the stupidity and pride of Piero might bring ruin
on his family, as eventually happened. Meanwhile, the advice he gave to
Piero could scarcely have been better conceived:

> When together with other youths of the ambassadors bear thyself
> sedately, politely, and kindly, towards thy equals. Be careful not to
> take precedence of those who are thine elders, for although thou art
> my son, thou art but a citizen of Florence, as they are . . . I send
> thee with Giovanni Tornabuoni, whom thou art to obey in all things
> and not to presume to do aught without him. Be modest and kindly
> in manner towards him and every one, and strive to bear thyself
> with sedateness, all the more that sedateness is not a youthful virtue.
> The honours and flatteries that will be bestowed upon thee will be a
> great danger if thou art not discreet and rememberest who thou
> art.[3]

But it was on his second son, Giovanni, that his hopes were chiefly
placed. In keeping with the peculiar custom of the time, Giovanni had
the archbishopric of Aix-en-Provence conferred on him in 1483,
although he was only seven, and in 1489 Lorenzo's persistent intrigues
succeeded in having him created a Cardinal. Writing to Giovanni on his
first visit to Rome wearing the scarlet hat, Lorenzo said:

> On this your first visit to Rome I think you had better make more
> use of your ears than your tongue. Today I have given you entirely
> to the Lord God and to Holy Church; therefore you must become a
> good priest and make it clear to everyone that you love the honour
> and state of Holy Church and the Apostolic See more than all else
> in this world. With this reserve, you should not lack opportunities
> for helping the city and our House; for it is for the good of the city
> to be united with the Church and in this you ought to be a valuable
> link and our House goes with the city. It is impossible to foresee the
> future, but, on the whole, I believe there will be plenty of ways, to
> quote the proverb, of saving the goat with the cabbages, but you
> must hold firmly to my first point of putting the Church before all
> else.[4]

A great deal of advice given here and elsewhere in the letter is in keeping with the rules eventually prescribed in Baldassare Castiglione's *Corteggiano*, the great contemporary handbook of social *mores*, but it was always intended that Giovanni as a Cardinal was first of all to serve the interests of the Medici and he took with him to Rome his tutor, Michelozzo, the son of the architect who had designed the Medici Palace, and some of Lorenzo's intimate advisers.

Lorenzo's wife, Clarice, died in 1488, an event which was not thought of any great significance either in Florence or in the closer Medici circles. The ambassador from Ferrara cruelly recorded the way in which the news of her death was received:

I wrote that Madonna Clarice was ill. She died three days ago, but I did not send the news at once, as it did not seem to me of much importance. Now that I am despatching the courier with letters from Naples, I inform your Excellency.[5]

Lorenzo wrote of her death to Pope Innocent VIII in kindlier terms:

Sanctissime ac Beatissime Pater post Pedum oscula Beatorum Vestrorum — Too often am I obliged to trouble and worry your Beatitude with accidents sent by fortune and divine interposition, which as they are not to be resisted must be borne with patience. But the death of Clarice, which has just occurred, my most dear and beloved wife, has been and is so prejudicial, so great a loss, and such a grief to me for many reasons, that it has exhausted my patience and my power of enduring anguish, and the persecution of fortune, which I did not think would have made me suffer thus. The deprivation of such habitual and such sweet company has filled my cup and has made me so miserable that I can find no peace. Nought is left but to pray God that he may give me peace, and I have faith that in His infinite love He will alleviate my sorrow and not overwhelm me with so many disasters as I have endured during these last years. I humbly beg Your Beatitude with all my heart to pray for me as I know how efficacious are such prayers. I commend myself and place myself at Your Holy Feet.

— Filetta, 31 July 1488.
Your devoted servant,
LAURENTIUS DE MEDICIS.[6]

But Clarice remains one of the unhappiest figures in the charmed circle. She could never come to terms with Lorenzo's humanist attitude to life or his coterie of scholars and wits — Matteo Franco was the only one whom she did not detest — and even within a short time after her wedding she had written to her husband in a petulant fashion:

> I should be glad not to be turned into ridicule by Franco in the same way as Luigi Pulci, nor to hear that Messer Angelo can say that he will stay in your house against my will, and that you have given him your own room at Fiesole. You know that I said that if you wished him to remain I would be content, and though he has called me a thousand names, if it is with your approval, I will endure it, but I cannot believe that it is true.[7]

Poor Clarice. But time was running out for Lorenzo. The Florentines were great believers in omens and the death of the famous giraffe in January 1489 seemed a portent. The giraffe had been sent a year earlier as a gift from the Sultan of Egypt and had been adopted by the citizens. It was seven braccias high and excited great curiosity, even among the nuns, and had to be sent round the convents to be inspected. It was said to be so tame that it would eat an apple from a child's hand, and fires were lit to keep it warm in winter. The giraffe must have been a source of some embarrassment to Lorenzo, but the death of a favourite is always mourned.

So ebullient a person as The Magnificent could scarcely be cabin'd within the confines of a few historical chapters and his versatility in different directions is displayed elsewhere in this book, but his remaining time can be briefly described.

His last two years were clouded by the hostile activity of Girolamo Savonarola. The asceticism, the aggressive puritanism, the memento mori preached by Savonarola were partly derived from his own personality; they were also the inevitable reaction against the liberty and licence of Lorenzo's earlier years. Savonarola's original preaching had been rejected by Florence and he spent several years wandering in Northern Italy, but it was Lorenzo who had called him to preach his reforming sermons again in Florence. All Savonarola's doctrines were alien to Medici humanism, but Lorenzo appreciated the force of his character and treated him with remarkable magnanimity. When Savonarola was elected Prior of the monastery of San Marco, he refused, as had been the custom, to pay a complimentary visit to Lorenzo in whose patronage the appointment lay. Lorenzo confined himself to the comment: 'Here is a stranger who has come into my house and will not deign even to visit me.'

Lorenzo was the real Magnificent figure of the Renaissance. He brought to Florence many classical and literary treasures – and did so just in time before the effect of the fall of Constantinople began to become apparent. While still only twenty-three, in 1472, he founded the University at Pisa and worked there himself for some time, but it was in Florence that his great work on behalf of learning was done. Latin was taught at Pisa, but in Italy only at Florence was Greek taught, and to the Greek Academy came celebrated scholars from all over Europe. Lorenzo's zeal for learning remained undiminished and his dying words to Poliziano and Pico della Mirandola were: 'I wish that death had spared me till I had completed your libraries.' Lorenzo died of gout, a hereditary affliction which greatly troubled many members of the Medici family. Sulphur baths, a popular prescription, eventually gave him no relief, and contemporary medical science was so backward that the celebrated Milanese doctor, Lazaro da Ficino, was, at the time of his death, treating Lorenzo with a mixture of crushed pearls and precious stones.

Poliziano gives a moving account of the death of his friend and patron in a letter to Jacopo Antiquario:

As soon as he saw me he called me to him and asked what Pico della Mirandola was doing. I replied that Pico had remained in town fearing to molest him with his presence. 'And I,' said Lorenzo, 'but for the fear that the journey here might be irksome to him would be most glad to see him and speak to him for the last time before I leave you all.' I asked if I should send for him. 'Certainly, and with all speed,' answered he. This I did, and Pico came and sat by the bed, whilst I leaned against his knees in order to hear the languid voice of my lord for the last time. With what goodness, with what courtesy, I may say with what caresses, Lorenzo received him. First he asked his pardon for thus disturbing him, begging him to regard it as a sign of the friendship – the love – he bore him, assuring him that he died more willingly after seeing so dear a friend. Then introducing, as was his wont, pleasant and familiar sayings, he joked also with us. 'I wish,' he said to Pico, 'that death had spared me until your library had been complete.' Pico had hardly left the room when Fra Girolamo [Savonarola] of Ferrara, a man celebrated for his doctrine and his sanctity and an excellent preacher, came in.[8]

There are varying accounts of Savonarola's last words to the dying

Lorenzo. According to some, he demanded that Lorenzo should confess and repent his responsibility for the sack of Volterra; his financial plundering of the public purse; and his debauching of the State: all of which Lorenzo declined. But most will agree that Poliziano's version is to be preferred:

> To his exhortations to remain firm in his faith and to live in future, if God granted him life, free from crime, or if God so willed it to receive death willingly, Lorenzo answered that he was firm in his religion, that his life would always be guided by it, and that nothing could be sweeter to him than death, if such was the divine will. Fra Girolamo then turned to go when Lorenzo said: 'Oh Father, before going deign to give me thy benediction.' Bowing his head, immersed in piety and religion he repeated the words and the prayers of the friar, without paying any attention to the grief now openly shown of his attendants. It seemed that all, save Lorenzo, were going to die, so calm was he. He gave no signs of anxiety or of sorrow; even in that supreme moment he showed his usual strength of mind and his fortitude. The doctors who stood round, not to seem idle, worried him with their remedies and assistance. He submitted to everything they suggested, not because he thought it would save him, but in order not to offend any one, even in death. To the last he had such mastery over himself that he joked about his own death. Thus when given something to eat and asked how he liked it he replied: 'As well as a dying man can like anything.' He embraced us all tenderly and humbly asked pardon if during his illness he had caused annoyance to any one. Then disposing himself to receive extreme unction he commended his soul to God. The Gospel containing the Passion of Christ was then read and he showed that he understood by moving his lips, or raising his languid eyes, or sometimes moving his fingers. Gazing upon a silver crucifix inlaid with precious stones and kissing it from time to time, he expired. . .
>
> — Fiesole, 18 May 1492.[9]

Savonarola had said that Lorenzo had occupied the people with tournaments and feasts so that they might think of themselves and not of him. At this distance, however, it seems likely that not only supporters of the Medici could agree with the humbler chronicler, Dei, who said that the splendour not of Tuscany only but of the whole of Italy had disappeared. The company of the Magi laid his body in the sacristy of San Lorenzo and, the day after, the funeral services took place without pomp, as was the custom for nobles, but simply, devoid of hangings and canopies, with three orders of friars and only one of priests, 'for no matter how pompous the ceremony might have been, it would always have proved too mean for so great a man.'[10]

There was nothing affecting Florence that Lorenzo had not touched. In external affairs he had maintained the independence of the state — not only by his embassy to the King of Naples during the Papal war and by continuing Cosimo's policy of keeping a balance of power between the city-states. He had also succeeded in surrounding Florence with a ring of friendly satellites, from Rimini to Siena. Machiavelli, writing later, did not approve of this approach which he believed militated against the chances of ever achieving a united Italy. Machiavelli had, however, to admit that there were few signs of a military spirit in Florence. This, he thought, was due to the loss of potential leaders after the downgrading of the nobles in 1293. It is the measure of Lorenzo's achievement that he was able to pursue his foreign policy successfully without the support of any permanent military resources. None of the Medici were trained as soldiers.

Lorenzo had less appetite than Cosimo for the machinations of government, but he had to rule. He had no alternative. He was by descent too important to be left to the pleasures of the countryside which he enjoyed so much. The Medici power was not a constitutional one: it was personal to the family. It is significant that the Pazzi tried to eliminate not only Lorenzo but his brother as well. One victim would not suffice; the survivor — as it happened, Lorenzo himself — could continue the Medici rule.

The manipulation of power, so dear to Cosimo's heart, was continued in a more open form under Lorenzo. The rewards of office went to Medici supporters and it was made clear that everything flowed from Lorenzo's favour.

He was happy with his family, although his marriage to Clarice was a state alliance and his relations with her became increasingly distant. Perhaps it was this that moved him to take such an extraordinary interest in the matrimonial affairs of his fellow Florentines. No one of any significance could wed without his permission and he was known to stop marriages of which he disapproved. He was faithful for lengthy periods to his succession of mistresses but it was in the company of artists and poets that he was most at home. A patron of artists, he was regarded by authors as a fellow-writer and he could match their talent.

It is his boundless Renaissance vitality that makes him so difficult to comprehend. A successful diplomat, his literary tastes ranged from earthy ballads to religious verse. He was steeped in Platonism, but could throw it aside and live entirely in the moment. He was devoted to country pursuits but loved the carnival processions and masques in the city. Falconry requires a strong nerve and a keen eye. Lorenzo had both, and perhaps the most characteristic picture would show him bringing the falcon back to the lure in the setting he described in his own *La caccia*. It is no wonder that he did not find time to be vindictive towards his enemies and in him the humanity and generosity of the Medici reached its highest.

Notes

1. F. Guicciardini, *History of Florence,* ed. J.R. Hale (Richard Sadler and Brown Ltd., London, 1966).
2. Janet Ross, *Lives of the Early Medici as told in Their Correspondence* (Chatto and Windus, London, 1910).
3. Ibid.
4. L. Collinson-Morley, *The Early Medici* (George Routledge and Sons Ltd., London, 1935).
5. Yvonne Maguire, *The Women of the Medici* (George Routledge and Sons Ltd., London, 1927).
6. Ross, *The Early Medici.*
7. Maguire, *The Women of the Medici.*
8. Ross, *The Early Medici.*
9. Ibid.
10. Guido Biagi, *The Private Life of the Renaissance Florentines* (Unwin, London, 1896).

5 ANGELO POLIZIANO

By the time of the Pazzi conspiracy Poliziano was one of Lorenzo's closest confidants, but the sad events that followed it led to a reversal in his career from which he never fully recovered. It was not only Poliziano's own position that was affected. The happenings which followed in quick succession — the murder of Giuliano in the Cathedral on 26 April 1478 (the anniversary of Simonetta's death); the excommunication of Florence in June; the outbreak of plague in the city; and the formal declaration of war during July — all seemed to conspire to bring to the surface the violent emotions and reactions which the Medici had succeeded in suppressing by wise, unobtrusive government under Cosimo and by the diversifications and entertainments constantly provided by Lorenzo. But after the summer of 1478 Lorenzo's motto of 'Le Temps Revient' no longer seemed so appropriate, and for Poliziano more than anyone else the springtime had disappeared.

Until this year, Poliziano had been prospering. He was in constant attendance on Lorenzo at the Medici Palace, at his country villas, and at the carnival processions which were frequently to be seen crowding through the narrow streets of Florence. He was no great lover himself — it was much later that he became affected by the charms of Alessandra Scala — but many of the ballads and other lyrics which he wrote at this time to match Lorenzo's own interest were highly licentious. His passion for this form of verse, and the enthusiasm he developed for the *trionfi* and masquerades are not only contemporary; they are like the enthusiasm for ribald rhymes and delight in pageantry still manifested by an otherwise respectable Oxford Don attending a Gaudy.

Poliziano was now a more substantial figure. He succeeded in extracting from his patron the gift of the Priory of San Paolo; the duties attached to the office were sufficiently undemanding to be performed by a substitute and there was an annual stipend of a hundred florins. Poliziano was able, as a dutiful son, to help his family and his mother had remarried. He could look with equanimity on the delights around him. He could concentrate on his ephemeral verses, on more lasting works like the *Stanze* commemorating Simonetta, and on expeditions with Lorenzo. Two particularly happy letters from this period have survived. Both are written to Clarice to report her husband's movements; both are utterly free from the playful pedantry that mars some of his later letters; and both illustrate admirably a carefree form of existence on which Poliziano was later to look back with some nostalgia. The first describes a hawking expedition — always one of Lorenzo's favourite pursuits:

Magnifica Domina mea — I did not write yesterday to Your Magnificence because Lorenzo sent me to Lucca. I have just come back and take up my pen to keep faith with you. Lorenzo is well and in good spirits. Yesterday as there was but little wind he went hawking; but they had not much luck because the young falcon belonging to Pilato, called the Mantuan, was lost. This morning they went out again, but the wind was not favourable, nevertheless we saw some fine flights, and Maestro Giorgio flew his Peregrine falcon which came back to the lure most obediently. Lorenzo is quite in love with it. Of a truth he is not wrong, for Maestro Giorgio says he never saw a handsomer or a better, and declares he will make of him the finest falcon in the world. While we were in the fields Pilato came back from the river with his lost falcon, so Lorenzo was doubly pleased. If I knew what to write I should be glad: but I can only give you news of his hawking as we do nought else in the fore- and the afternoon. This evening I hear that on Monday Lorenzo intends to hunt roe deer and then to return at once to Florence. Please God we may find you well and with a boy in your arms. I commend myself to Your Magnificence — In Pisa, 1 December 1475.
Make my excuses to Madonna Lucrezia if I have not written to her, but I have nought to say save what I write to you. Commend me to her.

Your servant,
AGNOLO DA MONTEPULCIANO.[1]

The prayer for a boy was duly answered by the birth on 11 December of Giovanni (afterwards Pope Leo X).

The second describes a light-hearted observation of Lent — perhaps not sufficiently grave to please the more pious Clarice:

Magnifica Domina mea — Yesterday after leaving Florence we came as far as San Miniato [al Tedesco], singing all the way, and occasionally talking of holy things so as not to forget Lent. At Lastra [a Signa] we drank *zappolino*, which tasted much better than I had been told. Lorenzo is brilliant and makes the whole company gay: yesterday I counted twenty-six horses of those who are with him.

When we reached San Miniato yester evening we began to read a little of S. Augustine, then the reading resolved itself into music, and looking at and instructing a certain well-known dancer who is here. Lorenzo is just going to Mass. I will finish another time — At San Miniato, 8 April (1476). Servitor.

YOUR AGNOLO[2]

In August 1478 Lorenzo decided that, with the plague still raging, and the outbreak of hostilities, Florence was not safe for his family and so Clarice and her children, accompanied by Poliziano as tutor, were despatched to safety at Pistoia. An early letter from Poliziano is already full of a sense of unease and the first signs of friction with Clarice. (In this letter, the Bartolommeo Sozzino mentioned was one of the masters of canon law who were asked to advise whether, despite the Pope's excommunication, Church services could still be held in the city.)

Agnolo Poliziano at Pistoia to Lorenzo de' Medici in Florence.
Magnifice mi patrone — I hope and trust Your Magnificence has not been disturbed by my letter written this morning under the influence of anger; the want of patience is my great fault. I hope in *bonam partem acceperis rebusque nostris prospectum curabis.*

Madonna Clarice sends you three pheasants and a partridge. She says you are to beware as though they came from an enemy because she does not know the man who brought them; he is the father of your Pisan courier who broke his leg.

By the bearer I send you the opinion of Messer Bartolommeo Sozzino. Every hour I have been entreating him to finish it and found a copyist who made all the haste he could, but it was impossible to get it done quicker.

Piero is well and I take every care of him, all the others are also in good health; but I get all the kicks; yet *te propter Libyeae.* I am longing for news that the plague has ceased on account of my anxiety for you and in order to return and serve you; for I hoped and I thought to be with you; but as you have, or rather my evil fortune has assigned to me this post in the service of Your Magnificence, I endure it, *quamvis durum, nec levius fit patientia.* I commend myself to Your Magnificence — Pistoia, 24 August 1478.[3]

Only two days later a petulant note appears when Poliziano writes to Lorenzo:

> I look after Piero and incite him to write; in a few days I think he will write to you in a fashion that will astonish you, we have here a master that teaches writing in fifteen days, he is excellent at his trade. The children play about more than usual and are in splendid health. God help them and you. Piero never leaves me or I him. I wish I had to serve you in some greater thing, but as this has fallen to my lot I do it willingly. *Rogo tamen, ut aliquid aut literarum aut nuntii huc perlatum ivi cures, desque operam, ne quidquid est in me auctoritatis, patriaris exolescere, quo et puerum facilius in officio teneam, et meo munere, ut par est defungar. Sed haec si commodum; fin minus, quod fors feret, feremus aequo animo.* Be of good cheer and take courage, for great men are formed by adversity. *Durate, et vosmet rebus servate secundis.* I commend myself to you – Pistoia, 26 August 1478. Your servant,
>
> ANG. POL.[4]

There is, incidentally, something absurd in the timid Poliziano urging his resolute master to take courage. It was, however, becoming clear that Clarice and Poliziano were in no sense compatible and it is difficult to dispute the suggestion made by Alan Moorehead in his splendidly succinct essay on Poliziano in *The Villa Diana* that the phrases in Latin were deliberately inserted because Clarice would not understand them even if they came to her notice.

A week later Poliziano writes tartly that 'Mona Clarice is very well; but takes little pleasure in aught save any good news we get from Florence. She rarely goes out.'[5] At the end of September he would report in favourable terms of the progress made by his charge, Lorenzo's son Piero, but there is an undercurrent of anxiety and what – in view of the earlier letters – would appear to be an unnecessary rehearsal of how much he owed to Lorenzo:

> Piero continues to learn to write and will soon be so good a penman that I hope he will relieve me of the trouble of writing *sine argumento* as I do now to you, so that I am ashamed of myself. But it may please God that I shall always have to write the same words to you, which are that we are all well. Madonna Clarice is much happier and better in health. We keep good guard and watch here, but we are anxious about you. God keep you, for it seems to me that all

depends upon that. Have no fear about us, for we are very careful. As far as I am concerned neither care nor goodwill shall be wanting. I know how much I owe to Your Magnificence, and the love I bear to Piero and to your other children is hardly second to your own. If anything unpleasant and unkind does sometimes happen I shall endeavour to bear it for love of you, *cum omnia debeo.* I commend myself to you — Pistoia, 20 September 1478.

AGNOLO POLIZIANO[6]

By the autumn Pistoia was no longer considered sufficiently safe, and the family had to move further north to the Medici villa at Caffagiuolo, fifteen miles from Florence. Here was nothing for comfort. The villa lies low in the Mugello valley. It is damp and cold and difficult of access. Pistoia had provided at least a bare minimum of civilised diversions, including the library of Maestro Zambino in which Poliziano found some interesting Latin and Greek texts. But, at Caffagiuolo, there was not even a neighbouring village. And it rained. Clarice was soon writing to her mother-in-law in terms of objective complaint: 'On account of the bad roads and the much rain we have not sent in the carrier for three days . . . We by God's grace are all quite well but in the water above our heads.'

In December Poliziano, too, wrote a sad letter to Lucrezia. It had rained incessantly and he could not leave the villa. The children had taken to playing ball for exercise. Poliziano remained huddled by the fire in his slippers and raincoat and Lucrezia, if she saw him, would think he was melancholy personified. They had heard rumours that the plague had ceased, so that the family might return to Florence, but the reports had proved false and increased his gloom. Poliziano himself was 'drowned in weary sloth' and solitude — not helped by the uncommunicative presence of Gentile Becchi, Bishop of Arezzo, who had joined the household. He ends the letter in near despair:

I remain alone, and when I am tired of study I ring the changes on plague and war, on grief for the past and fear for the future, and have no one with whom to air my phantasies. I do not find my Madonna Lucrezia in her room with whom I can unbosom myself and I am bored to death. Our sole relief is in letters from Florence, from Malerba, who has written these last few days, but I must tell you he generally sends good news which we believe for a little while, such is our desire that they may be true. But these plums usually turn into sloes. However I am trying to arm myself with hope and cling to everything in order not to sink to the bottom. I have nought else to say. I commend myself to Your Magnificence — Cafaggiuolo, 18 December 1478. *Servitor*

ANGELUS[7]

Meanwhile, in addition to his intolerable ennui, Poliziano was finding relations with Clarice increasingly difficult. There probably was little chance that this relationship could ever have been amicable. Clarice was a Roman Orsini, a devout orthodox Catholic and, as a result, she looked on Lorenzo's excommunication and the war with the Pope with the utmost misgivings. She was not particularly intelligent: she had no accomplishments to match those of her mother-in-law. She was dismayed at Lorenzo's love affairs and his preoccupation with masques, banquets and scurrilous verses, in which she had no part. And she would not have been human if she had not regarded the free-thinking, sarcastic, sharp-tongued Poliziano as one of those who encouraged Lorenzo in ways which she found entirely unsympathetic. She hated him accordingly. And, to make her more testy and irritable, she was exiled in the same house as her enemy, and she was heavily pregnant.

Clarice went to Florence for the birth of her child (Giuliano, after Lorenzo's brother) in February. She seems to have left Alberto di Malerba, a priest, behind to ensure that her sons, Piero and Giovanni, were not too influenced by Poliziano's heretical teaching. This was but one domestic and intimate application of the Renaissance conflict between the classics and Christianity; and the bitterness of this particular squabble shows how difficult it must have been to reach anything resembling a compromise. This is the clear implication of Poliziano's letter, written on 6 April 1479, to his distant patron:

> As for Giovanni, you will have seen for yourself. His mother has taken it upon herself to change his course of reading to the Psalter, a thing I did not approve of. While she was absent he had made wonderful progress. He was already able to select, without any help from me, all the letters and syllables in his exercise in composition.
>
> My only petition to God is that I may be able to prove to you some day my loyalty, diligence, and patience. This I would willingly purchase even at the expense of death.
>
> I omit much lest I should weary your busy mind.
>
> Farewell and remember me with all the rest — From Cafaggiuolo,

6 April 1479.[8]

Poliziano was justified in regretting the interruption of the boys' classical studies, as is shown in two touching letters from Piero to his father about the present of a pony. But Clarice's patience was now too severely taxed and, of her own accord, she expelled Poliziano from Cafaggiuolo. It would be interesting to know how she dismissed him. Did she seek the support of Gentile Becchi and Alberto di Malerba and formally rebuke the tutor for his interference and Godless teaching, or did they have a noisy personal row when recrimination could no longer be tolerated? In the domestic atmosphere of Cafaggiuolo, the latter seems more likely, and Poliziano was forced to depart at once, leaving behind his books and manuscripts which were both his precious working equipment and the symbols of his authority.

His quarrel with Clarice was Poliziano's critical error. He may not have realised how much and how often he had humiliated her. He certainly underestimated her fury, and he failed to appreciate — as other favourites had done — that, however great his standing with his master and however affectionate their past relationship had been, he did not have the status to intervene between husband and wife. Poliziano had no plans; he could not return to Florence without permission; but he went straight to the Villa Careggi, the scene of many pleasant banquets and Platonic arguments in more peaceful times, which was at least nearer the city. From there he wrote in pathetic terms to Lorenzo:

> *Magnifice mi Domine* — I am here at Careggi, having left Cafaggiuolo by command of Madonna Clarice. The cause and the manner of my departure I should wish, indeed I beg of you as a grace, to explain by word of mouth, it is too long to write. When you have heard me I think you will admit that all the fault is not mine. Out of respect, and not wishing to come to Florence *praeter jussa tua*, I am here to await the commands of your Magnificence as to what I am to do, because I am yours even if the whole world was against me. If I have had but small success in serving you it was not that I did not serve with all my heart. I commend myself to Your Magnificence, at whose commands I am most entirely — Careggi, 6 May 1479. Ever Your Magnificence's servant,
>
> ANGELUS POL.[9]

But Lorenzo could not overtly side with Poliziano against his wife, for whom he had a cool, but enduring, affection. He seems to have made a perfunctory attempt at settling the quarrel by making Poliziano librarian at the Villa Medici at Fiesole, but Clarice was unappeased and complained bitterly that Poliziano's friends and fellow wits were ridiculing her. She refused to part with his papers, and Lorenzo found it necessary to pay a hurried visit to Cafaggiuolo. The outcome was that Poliziano was to have his belongings returned to him at Fiesole; but he was not to be reinstated as tutor. Clarice had gained nearly all her objectives.

Poliziano soon realised that, although he might retain Lorenzo's affection, though somewhat tempered by the trouble with Clarice, he had lost much of his own influence. He was no longer the daily companion: those who sought preferment at the Medici court did not now find it helpful to seek his support. He was suddenly a lonely figure and could not but realise how precarious his position was. In these times of adversity he applied himself – just as he had done in his youth – to his work on classical authors. He translated Plutarch and Epictetus, as though to give notice that his reputation and authority as a scholar were undiminished, and he started to reorganise the great collection of manuscripts in the Medici Library.

But he was still anxious to be restored to his position in the Medici household. Not that the prospects were bright, for Clarice had secured the appointment as tutor of Bernardo Michelozzo. Bernardo, the son of the architect, remained so close to the Medici family that, after Giovanni de' Medici became Pope Leo X, he was made Bishop of Forli and given permission to change his name and arms to those of the Medici. Poliziano's anxiety is very clear from a letter to Madonna Lucrezia written in July 1479:

I am also writing to Giovanni, to the children, and to their master. I pray you to give him the letters and to commend me to him, for I set great store and count much on the affection he shows me. I have been to see Lorenzo several times and cannot describe how well he received me. Do try and discover what are his intentions with regard to me; it would surprise me if Piero were allowed to lose time, it would be a great pity. I hear that Messer Bernardo, brother of Ser Niccolo is with him, but I do not know how his teaching will combine with mine. If he is to remain permanently, then of a truth I can assume that the bubble has burst. But I cannot believe it, and therefore beg you to find out what are Lorenzo's intentions, then I shall know whether I am to arm for a joust only or for war. It will

be easy for you and I shall always be at the beck and call of Lorenzo
as I am sure he knows better than I, and that he will put me in an
honourable position as he always has done and as my fidelity and
good services merit. I am working hard. Till now I have not been
able to send you the promised book as one copy is at Florence and
the other at the binder's who has kept it a long time. As soon as
I have it I will send it. I commend myself to you and I pray you to
commend me to Lorenzo — Fiesole, 18 July 1479. Your Magnificence's servant,

ANGELUS POLIZIANUS[10]

Poliziano's plaintive letter went unheeded. The time was not propitious. The war was going badly for Florence and Lorenzo had plenty
to think about. In September 1479 the Florentines had real cause for
alarm when Poggibonsi, near Siena, was captured by the enemy. The
way to Florence lay open and when the next attack was mustered by
the Papal troops their allies' resistance would become increasingly
difficult. (It is of interest that in the Second World War the Germans
fully realised the tactical desirability of holding Poggibonsi: it was the
scene of unusually bitter fighting and was captured and recaptured no
less than three times.) Faced with this peril to the state, Lorenzo took
his heroic decision to go to the court of the King of Naples, although
he was his enemy, and seek his support. If a mission of this kind was to
succeed it had to be kept small; it was not a formal embassy, although
for protocol purposes Lorenzo was declared an ambassador, and there
was no room for passengers. There was no room for Poliziano.

He was not a statesman or a diplomat. He was better at making
enemies than friends and, although he could claim to belong to the
brotherhood of scholars, his sharp tongue and acid wit would not have
served Lorenzo well on his hazardous expedition. His epigrams on
Neapolitan manners and behaviour would hardly have endeared the
Florentines to the court of the King. Although Lorenzo's decision to
go to Naples was taken suddenly and acted on with despatch, there
were inevitably rumours that a dramatic move was afoot and reports
soon reached Fiesole. Poliziano had no great zest for placing himself in
a situation as dangerous as the Naples voyage was likely to be, but —
this was his dreadful dilemma — he could not face the indignity of
being left behind by the Magnificent. He sought the support of
Madonna Lucrezia; he wrote to Lorenzo; he, the former favourite and
intimate confidant, suffered the indignity of having to importune
admission to the Palazzo Medici. But he met with no success. His

ultimate humiliation was to be denied access to his patron. After a final meeting with the Signoria, Lorenzo departed without him. It seems likely that Lorenzo's slightly callous decision was taken on severely practical grounds: he always knew what his priorities were and he knew that this was a time for harsh reality, not for wit or learning.

This was the nadir of Poliziano's career at the Medici court. There were rumours spread about by those who had no reason to like him that he was too cowardly to accompany his patron to Naples. There were others who were not displeased that he was now completely discredited. Clarice had her moment of triumph and there is no record of her extending any compassion to the former tutor. Imprudently, in a mixture of despair and indignation, Poliziano left Fiesole and went to the neutral town of Bologna. His critics said that this was treason — to desert the city in time of distress — and confirmed their worst suspicions of him. Poliziano spent the next few painful months in an aimless fashion in the cities of the Lombardy plain, particularly in Mantua where he secured employment for a time with Cardinal Gonzaga. He was soon overcome with remorse that, partly by his own action, he had placed himself outside the charmed circle. For, in March 1480, Lorenzo returned in triumph and the war was over.

Poliziano at once addressed a stream of letters to Florence. They were a mixture of congratulation, self-justification, and supplication. For a time there was no response; even acknowledgement arrived only at second hand, and Poliziano began to contemplate spending the rest of his life in exile. But, as has already been noticed elsewhere in this book, a surprising magnanimity is one of the most prominent Medici characteristics, and five months later Lorenzo summoned Poliziano back to Florence. He was reappointed tutor to Piero and, of more lasting importance, made Professor of Latin and Greek at the Studio Fiorentino. Throughout the middle ages and the Renaissance, the idea of the wheel of fortune bringing both retribution and rewards was not seen as an empty cliché. It was thought to be a real motive force, and the latest turn of the wheel was more to Poliziano's advantage than he had imagined possible.

Lorenzo may have thought that a return to the carnival days, at least in a modified and less irresponsible way, was now in prospect and that he wanted his familiar back in his court. But a more probable explanation is that Lorenzo was perceptive enough to realise that Poliziano's real virtue lay, not in rhymes, ballads or epigrams, but in his unrivalled scholarship. Poliziano had reacted to his two main reverses by seeking consolation in his studies. Lorenzo wanted to consolidate and advance the arrangements for the pursuit of learning and, for this purpose, Poliziano was his man. This coincidence of interest and intent on the part of the patron and the professor was a happy event for European scholarship.

It is tempting to think of Poliziano from now on as a reformed rake. But this scarcely seems to have been so. There were still libidinous verses from time to time and even towards the end of his life he was ill-advisedly pursuing Alessandra Scala. But it was as a scholar, as a proponent and interpreter of the classics, that he advanced his reputation. He was not only a scholar; now that he was free to concentrate on his studies he developed a new eloquence derived from his profound knowledge of his subject. The audiences at the Studio grew in number and he set a tradition as a lecturer in the humanities which his successors over the centuries found it hard to emulate. Lorenzo had given him the Villa Bruscoli (now called the Villa Diana) so evocatively described by Alan Moorehead in his monograph. There he wrote his main treatise on the classical poets — the *Sylvae*, of which an account is given in Chapter 7. This is a work of rounded scholarship and by itself shows how wise Lorenzo had been in summoning Poliziano back to the city.

Studies of new texts, lectures, a growing friendship with Pico della Mirandola, initial encouragement for the young Michelangelo. These were halycon years for Poliziano. In 1484 he escorted Piero de' Medici, with whom he had a long association, to Rome and presented the Pope with a translation of Herodian. Four years later he again accompanied Piero to the Eternal City for his marriage to Alfonsina Orsini. En route he wrote to Lorenzo in terms reminiscent of earlier years:

Magnifice Domine mi — We arrived safely at Acquapendente yester evening at 8 o'clock, I wrote to you also from Montepulciano. Tomorrow we leave for Viterbo. We are all in high spirits and find good cheer, and all along the road we pick up new tunes and May songs, which seem to me more original here than elsewhere, *alla Romanesca, vel nota ipsa vel argumento*. I commend myself to your Magnificence — Acquapendente, 2 May 1488. Your Magnificence's servant,

ANG. POLITIANUS.[11]

Apart from these occasional diplomatic missions — and the two to Rome arose from his responsibility for Piero's education — his journeys

from Florence were now infrequent and mainly concerned with the
acquisition of books and manuscripts. A letter to Lorenzo in 1491 is
typical:

> MAGNIFICENT PATRON — My last letter was from Ferrara. In
> Padua I found some good books, *i.e.* Simplicio, on the Sky; Ales-
> sandro, on the Topica; Giovan Grammatico, on the Posteriora and
> the Syllogism; a David on Aristotle; none of which we have in
> Florence. I also found a Greek scribe in Padua and arranged with
> him at a ducat for every fifteen pages.
>
> Maestro Piero Leoni showed me his books: among them I found
> M. Manlio, an old astronomer and poet, which I have brought with
> me to Venice to compare with one I have bought; I have never seen
> a more ancient book. *Similiter* he possesses certain books of Galieno
> *de dogmate Aristotelis et Hippocratis* in Greek, of which he will
> give us a copy in Padua, so we shall have gained something.
>
> In Venice I have found some books of Archimedes and Eron,
> mathematicians, which we have not got, and a Frunuto *de Deis*, and
> other valuable things. So papa Janni will have writing enough to do
> for some time.[13]

'Papa Janni' was a Greek scribe employed by Lorenzo in copying.

Happy in his work, his friends, his benefices, and above all in the
continued support of his patron, Poliziano could reflect that — as the
second epitaph placed on his tomb in San Marco was later to record —
the Athens of Pericles was rising again in the Florence of the Magnificent.
The only sombre shadows were cast by Lorenzo's failing health and the
growing influence of Savonarola. The doctrines of the Dominican
monk were completely antipathetic to the humanism which had been
Poliziano's religion, and the hysterical support which Savonarola was
gradually rousing seemed to him to be the work of a hostile power.

In March 1492 Lorenzo was failing rapidly. He was scarcely able to
attend the ceremonies at the Medici Palace to celebrate the elevation
of his son Giovanni to be a Cardinal. Soon after, he was brought back
to die at Careggi. Poliziano's happy universe was destroyed almost overnight. Apart from his own grief, eloquently expressed in his account
of Lorenzo's last hours (Chapter 4), everything he believed in was
rapidly beginning to crumble. He lived for another two years in an
atmosphere of deepening gloom. His pupil, Piero, proved a hopeless
ruler and was soon expelled by the fury of the Florentines. Almost
overnight Poliziano belonged to a bygone age. The Palazzo Medici was

looted and the library was dispersed. His friends, too, were failing, and Poliziano would take refuge only in his own stoic philosophy. He was the last of Lorenzo's circle to be converted to Savonarola's doctrine, and it is impossible to believe that his expressed wish to be received into the Dominican order and to be buried as a friar was made in anything but hopeless resignation. His whole habit of thought was too different from Savonarola's to make a real reconciliation possible. The same is true of his friend, Pico della Mirandola, who died a few weeks later and was also interred at Santa Croce.

In many ways Poliziano was the chief glory of the Medici circle — as a wit, as a poet of great fluency and skill in the native Italian tongue, and as the leading scholar of his day. No account of fifteenth-century Florence can fail to recognise his eminence and his influence over the whole humanist scene. As a person he remains enigmatic. He aroused Lorenzo's affection, but elsewhere he was as likely to find enemies as friends. And he demonstrated the advantages, the attractions, and the pitfalls of one who puts his trust in princes.

Notes

1.   Janet Ross, *Lives of the Early Medici as told in Their Correspondence* (Chatto and Windus, London, 1910).
2.   Ibid.
3.   Ibid.
4.   Ibid.
5.   Ibid.
6.   Ibid.
7.   Ibid.
8.   Ibid.
9.   Ibid.
10.   Ibid.
11.   Ibid.
12.   Ibid.

6 PICO DELLA MIRANDOLA

The most meteorlike, and in some ways the most unusual, of Lorenzo's large company of scholars was Pico della Mirandola, although, in the last resort, it is his attitude and his promise that are remembered more than his actual achievements. Like Hamlet, his obituary might be that he was likely, had he been put on, 't'have proved most royally'. Walter Pater concluded last century that many Renaissance figures were more significant for what they set out to do than for what they succeeded in doing, and Pico adds much colour to this theory.

Born on 24 February 1463, Pico was the youngest son of a minor Italian prince, Giovanni Francesco Pico, Lord of Mirandola, a small territory near Ferrara which was subsequently absorbed in the Duchy of Modena. Pico is demonstrably from Picus, the nephew of the Emperor Constantine, from whom, like his ancestors, he claimed to be descended. The mystical air which surrounded Pico throughout his life was apparent at the very outset. A strange portent in the form of a circular flame was said to have appeared from the wall of the chamber at the moment when his mother gave him birth. This was alleged to denote the arrival of someone with supernatural powers, and it is true that Pico was always interested in the occult sciences. A forthright independence was also an unmistakable family characteristic. Pico's elder brother, Galeotto, for example, a successful soldier who succeeded his father to administer the ancestral estates, roused admiration among his contemporaries for the unusual feat of defying a papal excommunication. This he did successfully — and with contemptuous ease — for a period of sixteen years until his death. Pico's subsequent troubles with the Holy See may have been exacerbated by displeasure at his brother's conduct.

Pico's romantic character and extraordinary comeliness — in an age when male physical beauty was greatly esteemed — won him many friends. For this, and his great learning, he was described by his close friend, Poliziano, as 'omnium doctrinarum lux'. Machiavelli, whose own disposition was as far removed from Pico's as it could be, admitted that he was 'uomo quasiche divino'; and Savonarola, who persuaded him belatedly to joint the Dominican order, spoke of his ability and character with reluctant respect. But the best description of his effect on his contemporaries is that given by the scholarly Ficino recounting their first meeting in Florence. According to Ficino there appeared in his study an extraordinary-looking youth whose arrival coincided, almost symbolically, with the completion of Ficino's great work, his translation of Plato into Latin. In the words of Pico's nephew, Francesco, as translated by Sir Thomas More, Pico appeared 'of feature seemly and beauteous, of stature goodly and high, of flesh tender and soft, his visage lovely and fair, his colour white, intermingled with comely reds, his eyes grey, and quick of look, his teeth white and even, his hair yellow and abundant.'[1] To complete the picture, his hair was more elaborately dressed than was the normal custom.

And, since his eyes dazzled, he died young. Some accounts say that his death was brought about by a raging fever; others say that he was poisoned. Inevitably his demise had been the subject of prophecy — that he would die 'in the time of the lilies' — and his death at the age of thirty-two, early even by fifteenth-century standards, is recorded as taking place on 17 November 1494. He had foretold that he would not see old age: 'It is a happy thing, when heaven is friendly to us, to die young; to complete one day then is better than to wait until the evening.'[2]

If it appears that Pico was very like Mercutio to Lorenzo de' Medici's Romeo (and he had the same effervescence, ebullience and imaginative facility of expression as Mercutio) this would be a misleading impression. It is true that, in his youth, he wrote some books of erotic verse in Latin elegiacs — a common form of expression for the bloods of the day — which he subsequently destroyed, and a number of fairly indifferent sonnets in the vernacular which have survived. His basic habit of thought, however, was much more serious and more profound, and throughout his life his main preoccupations were with philosophy and theology. His education had prepared him thoroughly for this course.

He studied canon law at the University of Bologna from 1477 to 1479, then literature at Ferrara under the tutelage of Giambattista Guarino, but it soon became clear that his real interests lay in philosophical study and disputation, and the next four years at Padua and then at Pavia were so spent. In these years he amassed a famous library. He seems to have made intermittent visits to Florence during this time, and he certainly had met Ficino. About 1484 he stayed for a longer period in the city and soon became one of the most active members of the Platonic Academy.

It is easy to imagine him taking part in gatherings like an earlier one described by Ficino in his *Sopra l'Amore*, an exposition of Plato's

Symposium. (As a testimony to the author's versatility, it was written first in Latin and then translated into Italian.) Ficino describes in evocative terms the banquet at Lorenzo's villa at Careggi. It was held on 7 November, a date of some significance for the members of the Academy as it was said to mark the birth and death of Plato. Nine guests were invited to correspond to the nine muses and, to complete this elegant pastiche, after dinner the *Symposium* was read and discussed at leisure.

Platonism represented one half of Pico's interests; the other half consisted of sterner religious doctrines. After a visit to Paris in 1485, he returned the following year to Rome. He then set out for public debate and discussion his famous list of 900 propositions questioning many branches of philosophy and theology and touching also on magic and the Cabbalah. His theses were printed and circulated to universities, not only in Rome but throughout Italy. This was a remarkable thing to do. It showed unusual energy, a questioning mind and a very personal brand of courage. The actual content of the propositions matters less than the decision to produce them, to challenge orthodox doctrine and to invite examination. It is no wonder that his enemies, according to Jesup's *Life* (published in English in 1723) 'reputed him an introducer of Novelties.' The whole history of Renaissance Italy, from the youthful, ingenuous enthusiasms of its first years to the darker shades as it emerged into baroque, has no more surprising figure than the graceful nobleman, then twenty-three years old, who was only too willing to meet the Church on its own ground.

Pico had taken the precaution of obtaining the permission of Pope Innocent VIII before publishing his *Conclusions*. The initial astonishment which they aroused, however, soon gave way to envy and, according to Gresswell, Roman scholars soon made use of 'the lampoon and pasquinade, and such other literary weapons as timidity sheltered by secrecy could devise to discredit Pico.'[3] The Church authorities could not concede the possibility of debate, far less attempt to answer Pico's questions. There was no great public discussion as he had hoped, and he was compelled to sign a renunciation of thirteen of his *Conclusions* which were solemnly declared to be tainted with heresy.

The Roman Curia still regarded him as a potential danger and were unwilling to allow him to pursue his unorthodox theories at large. In the normal clandestine, intriguing manner of the time, the Church contrived to have him arrested during his second visit to France. For some time he was imprisoned in the Castle of Vincennes while the King of France, the Milanese ambassador, and the Apostolic Nuncio, sitting in uneasy conclave, decided what to do with their embarrassing prisoner. Pico published an *Apologia* demonstrating that his questions did not impugn his orthodoxy, but it was only due to the influence of his friend Lorenzo that Pope Alexander VI was persuaded to desist from further persecution. So much is clear from Lorenzo's correspondence with Giovanni Lanfredini, the Florentine ambassador at Rome:

> The Count della Mirandola is here leading a most saintly life, like a monk. He has been and is now occupied in writing admirable theological works: commentaries and Psalms; and other excellent books on theology. He recites the ordinary priest's office, observes all fasts and absolute chastity: has but a small retinue and lives quite simply with only what is necessary. To me he appears an example to other men. He is anxious to be absolved from what little contumacy is still attributed to him by the Holy Father and to have a Brief by which His Holiness accepts him as a son and a good Christian, he persevering in a Christian life. I greatly desire that this satisfaction should be given to him, for there are few men I love better or esteem more. I feel certain that he is a devout and faithful Christian, and his conduct is such that the whole city would vouch for him. Do all you can to obtain this Brief in such a form that it may content his conscience. This would be not less agreeable to me than any one of the many services you have rendered, and for which I am most grateful — 19 June 1489.[4]

Lorenzo's initial approach, however, met with less acceptance than his normal communications with the Holy See and he wrote again in terms which tell us as much of Lorenzo's character as of Pico's:

> Lorenzo de' Medici to Giovanni Lanfredini, Florentine Ambassador at Rome.
> To my great vexation I hear how this work of Mirandola's is abused, and were I not sure that such persecution is dictated solely by envy and malignity, by my faith, I should not mention it. The book has been examined by all the most learned priests here, well-known men of saintly life, and has been highly approved of by them as a Christian and a marvellous work. I am not so bad a Christian as to remain silent or to encourage him if I thought otherwise. I am certain that if he recited the *Credo* those spiteful men would say it was rank heresy. If His Holiness had the intelligence to understand this and was 1 ɔt too busy, I am sure these accusations would fall to the ground and

truth would prevail; but he is obliged to trust to others. This poor man is unable to defend himself because they say his premises are against His Holiness. If he had to contend with them only without the authority of the Pope to back them I am sure he would soon silence them. It is his misfortune to have to submit to the judgement of ignorant and malicious men who use the Pope as a shield. I have already told you that I believe all this is done with the intent to drive him to despair and cause him to lose his head so that eventually he should turn against the Pope; for believe me, Giovanni, he is one who could commit either great evil or great good. His life and character demonstrate this. If they drive him into another path I shall lose little, as I know that wherever he may be he will always bear me goodwill because of my great affection for him. I have never been able to make you understand this; and without entering into details, which I cannot do, I must tell you that he has been sorely tempted by something which might raise a great scandal, and I have always stopped him. Latterly he has been leading a saintly life here, and his mind is at rest. These devils with their persecutions will tempt him. People place far too much faith in them. In short I can only grieve over all this and beg you again to use all your cleverness in order to arrange matters, for you have no idea how it vexes and irritates me. If you knew how much, you would never rest until you have taken it off my mind – October 1489.[5]

It appears likely, however, that Lorenzo's last letter on this subject finally proved his case:

Lorenzo de' Medici to Giovanni Lanfredini, Florentine Ambassador at Rome.
Two days ago I met by chance the Count della Mirandola riding in the outskirts of Florence. He is living very quietly in a villa near by, immersed in his studies. He desires at last to know what his future is to be, for having obeyed His Holiness hitherto and being decided to obey him implicitly in the future, he wishes to have some indication that His Holiness accepts his obedience in the form of a Brief, whereby the Pope acknowledges him as an obedient son and a good Christian, which I believe him to be. Among other proofs of this he has converted a young Jew who has been translating for him from the Hebrew language, of which he is a perfect master, whom he has persuaded to become a Christian. This is not the act of a heretic. I much desire that for the honour of His Holiness and for

my own satisfaction this matter should be finished, and that the virtue and goodness of the said Count Giovanni should have as great a weight as the calumnies and suggestions of others. By nature he is devoted to His Holiness and does not dwell on what is past. Once delivered from this contumacy he will be the partisan and faithful servant of His Holiness, who to my thinking will thereby gain much — 11 August 1490.[6]

Pico spent the rest of his life in Florence and the Villa Querceto near Fiesole became his home. (In Renaissance Italy, the elegance of the villas on the hills round Florence was rivalled only by the accomplishments of their occupants — Poliziano, Ficino, Pico and many others — each encamped in a villa on a small Tuscan hill with a cypress-lined avenue leading up to it.) There Pico wrote his *Heptaplus*, a mystical account of the creation; his *De Ente et Uno*, a study of Plato and Aristotle; and he planned an elaborate sevenfold treatise against various forms of heresy and the enemies of the Church. Only one book, the *Disputationes adversus Astrologiam Divinatrichem* has survived. (Unlike many of his contemporaries, Pico was resolutely opposed to the study of Astrology.) His latter years were increasingly sombre, as they were for all the survivors from the Medici springtime. Lorenzo's death — and Pico and Poliziano were present at his last hours — deprived him of a patron, a fellow-Platonist and a close friend. He came increasingly under the influence of Savonarola who saw that the conversion of Pico would be a notable achievement. But Pico long hesitated to join the *Fratri Predicanti* and was not wildly enthusiastic when Savonarola prescribed the discipline of the scourge. Pico eventually sought entrance to the Dominican order. Savonarola's last word was somewhat lacking in Christian charity. In a public sermon at Santa Reparata, he claimed that it had been divinely revealed to him that Pico, while not in hell, was not in heaven either, but was languishing in purgatory for having so long delayed his admission to the Dominicans.

What was left when the bright meteor had burned itself out? That he stimulated others by his conversation is not in doubt. He may even have been one who, like Samuel Taylor Coleridge, was pre-eminently a talker. But, despite his great qualities of mind and his emotional attraction for his contemporaries, his works remain strangely inchoate. They are a mixture of scholastic theory, neo-Platonism and a taste for the occult. Pico's special contribution to this area was his study of the Cabbalah, using proper cabbalistic methods, for example numerical schemes of hidden meanings, to arrive at his interpretations. In some ways Pico exemplifies the limits to the progress which the New Learning had made in the course of the century, but his attack on the alleged occult influence of heavenly bodies (despite his own belief in natural magic) was influential.

His pure Platonic beliefs are best demonstrated in his *Platonick Discourse upon Love*. The *Discourse* takes the form of a commentary on a short poem by his close friend, Girolamo di Paolo Benivieni, whom he had first met on an earlier visit to Florence in 1479. In the second book of the *Discourse* he gives the clearest account of his theories on love and beauty − already set out by Ficino − which had so much attraction for many of the most scholarly minds of the Renaissance and appear later in the *Corteggiano* of Baldassare Castiglione. According to Pico, the most perfect human lovers are those

> that, remembering a more perfect Beauty than their souls saw of old, before they were fettered to the body, are kindled with an incredible desire of rebeholding that Beauty: and to the end that they may obtain this purpose, they sever themselves as much as they can from the body, in such fashion that the soul returneth to her pristine dignity, becoming entirely mistress of the body, and is no longer subject to it any wise. And then is the soul in that love which is the image of celestial love, and this alone is the human love that can be called perfect.

A more urbane philosophy was expressed in his letter from Paris of 15 October 1482 to Andrea Corneus:

> Philosophy is not an exercise for wit only, as is mistakenly suggested, for it enriches the understanding and lodges a treasure in the mind that will carry a man through all the vicissitudes of fortune, and without a change of countenance. The same thing is variously esteemed by different persons, and you may think it a Man's great happiness to live in the embraces of men of dignity and power, and in the plenty and splendour of the Court: but of these, you know, I have had my share, and can assure you I could never find a Regale for my soul in anything but retreat and contemplation; in which I hope to employ the time that shall remain to me.[7]

The great question for Renaissance philosophers was the harmonisation of Platonism and Christianity, and in this dispute Pico's great learning was used to good effect. According to Jesup, 'his reading and remarks were vastly more extensive than could be expected from so short a life.' In none of his writings does Pico give a systematic exposition of his philosophical thought, but the main tendencies are clear. From his works, and those of his contemporary Gianfrancesco Pico, it is known that their main objective was to reconcile Plato and Aristotle, theology and philosophy. According to Pico's version, the Universe is built of three orders of reality: the intellectual world of God and the angels; the celestial world ordained in ten spheres (the supreme one, the *coelum empireum*, being the mainspring of the universe); and the elementary world of the terrestrians. Man is a microcosm and is therefore formed by elements from all three orders and creates a world of his own. Pico held that the objects of philosophical knowledge and religious belief were identical. 'Philosophia veritatem quaerit, theologia invenit, religio possidet.' He was, as Walter Pater said, a true humanist. He believed that 'there was a spirit of order and beauty in knowledge' and that nothing which has ever interested mankind could lose its vitality.

His most famous doctrine was that concerning human freedom. Man is the only kind of being to stand outside the scale of orders of existence. He is accordingly not predetermined, as are all other kinds of being, to accept the limitations, powers and capacities that go along with a place on this scale. On the contrary, he has the freedom to rise or fall and his fate is dependent on his own efforts.

Jesup suggested that Pico had five basic virtues. First, there was his vast, natural genius; he was born with a talent which few have equalled. Secondly, it has to be admitted that he was much assisted by considerable wealth which enabled him to purchase a library valued at 7,000 ducats, a vast sum for the time. Thirdly, he had a natural bent for industry and application and, when his mind was so inclined, could accomplish surprising volumes of work. He learned Hebrew and Arabic in order to study philosophy and theology in as wide a context as possible. Next there was his memory:

'Twas observed, at his first appearance in the School, that his Fancy was Gay and Bright, his Wit strong and ready, and he had a Richness of Memory that had hardly been enjoy'd before him: For it was observ'd that, what he had but once heard, he would Repeat forward and backward without mistaking the least syllable.[8]

It is still the fashion in Italy (though, apparently, not elsewhere) for someone who has been asked a difficult question involving the exercise of powers of memory to reply indignantly, 'I am not Pico della Mirandola.' Lastly, there was his utter contempt for dignity and money. To the English reader he seems more like the Elizabethan scholars and blades, Greville and Walter Raleigh. And, like Raleigh, he might have said 'True love is a durable fyre.'

He is buried in the Church of San Marco, near his friend Poliziano, and the epitaph on his tomb, attributed to Hercules Strozza, reads:

JOHANNES. JACET. HIC. MIRANDOLA. CAETERA. NORUNT
ET. TAGUS. ET. ANGES. FORSAN ET ANTIPODES.

Notes

1. Walter Pater, *The Renaissance* (Macmillan, London, 1910).
2. Pico della Mirandola, *A Platonick Discourse upon Love*, E.G. Gardiner (ed.) (London, 1914).
3. W. Parr Gresswell, *Memoirs of Poliziano, Johannes Picus* etc. (Cadell and Davies, London, 1805).
4. Janet Ross, *Lives of the Early Medici as told in Their Correspondence* (Chatto and Windus, London, 1910).
5. Ibid.
6. Ibid.
7. E. Jesup, *The Lives of Picus and Pascal* (J. Hooke, London, 1723), p. 44.
8. Jesup, *Picus and Pascal*, p. 6.

7 THE MEDICI POETS

The poetry of the Medici springtime owes much to the relentless versatility of the accomplished Lorenzo, and if, in retrospect, his literary significance seems to lie most in the favourable conditions which he created for poets and authors rather than in his own writing, he still made his own mark. Politicians and their wives nowadays are, on occasion, known to write verses, but none would dare to set an entire literary fashion or seek to elevate the poet from the apathy with which he is now generally regarded. In Lorenzo's day, as a result of his personal influence and example, poets were highly esteemed, at least as highly as the great Florentine painters who were their contemporaries.

Lorenzo's literary reputation, however, does not depend solely on his skill as an organiser, as an impresario who could persuade bankers, statesmen and princes as well as poets to follow his own inclination. By his own writings he did much to ensure for the future the respectability of the Italian tongue as a literary medium. There had been a gap of many years since the poetry of Dante, Petrarch and Boccaccio; and the enthusiasm for the study and imitation of the classics, which had inspired the humanists, had led to contempt for native Italian. Poliziano, as we will see, first attracted attention for his Latin verses, and a facility in Latin and Greek elegiacs was thought to be essential for any ambitious author. Although more erudite than most merchant princes before or since, Lorenzo was not a pedant. He saw things in a different light and, throughout his career, he advocated and practised the use of the Italian language in poetry. In his enthusiasm he even claimed that Italian should be held equal to Latin and Greek and that Petrarch's works were superior to those of Ovid and the Latin lyricists.

It would be idle to ignore the political undertones of this attitude. A cardinal feature of the policy of the Medici family was to side with the people against the aristocrats, and what better way to obtain the people's favour than by composing popular songs in their own language? Lorenzo's attention to the rhythmic *canzoni a ballo* and *canti carnascialeschi* and his active promotion of the many masked carnival processions held throughout the year may have been due, at least in part, to a desire to divert the attention of the citizens from the

90

way in which the business of the state was conducted. That was
certainly Savonarola's view. Guicciardini made the same point in
gentler terms. He recorded that Lorenzo's death was 'a great sorrow to
the population of the city, and especially to the lower classes, always
kept by him in abundance, with many pleasures, entertainments and
feasts.'[1] But Guicciardini went on to say that Lorenzo's demise had
also 'grieved all those in Italy who excelled in letters, painting,
sculpture and similar arts'[2] either because he had commissioned their
works for fairly lavish rewards or because princes elsewhere in Italy
made more of artists than they would otherwise have done in order to
keep them from going off to Lorenzo. Whatever Lorenzo's motives
may have been, he enhanced the reputation of the Italian tongue and
set the scene for others.

Lorenzo's affection for the countryside, his delight in his country
villas at Careggi and Caiano, were fundamental to his character. He was
in many ways a very earthy man. All this is immediately apparent in
his poetry where he shows an uninhibited and genuine love of nature
and, as a corollary, a remarkable gift for lucid description. His rural
scenes are not invoked by inference: they are described for us in detail.
The fire of true poetic inspiration may be lacking; Lorenzo was too
analytical, and the Medici were always too detached, for that. But his
early sonnets have a grace of poetic description which makes them
worth more than a glance. The following sonnet in Symonds' translation shows, too, the progress which had been made in adapting the
study of the classics to the native tongue:

> Leave thy beloved isle, thou Cyprian queen;
>   Leave thy enchanted realm so delicate,
>   Goddess of love! Come where the rivulet
>   Bathes the short turf and blades of tenderest green!
> Come to these shades, these airs that stir the screen
>   Of whispering branches and their murmurs set
>   To Philomel's enamoured canzonet:
>   Choose this for thine own land, thy loved demesne!
> And if thou com'st by these clear rills to reign,
>   Bring thy dear son, thy darling son, with thee;
>   For there be none that own his empire here.
> From Dian steal the vestals of her train,
>   Who roam the woods at will, from danger free,
>   And know not Love, nor his dread anger fear.

But the limitations of Lorenzo's sonnets are easily exposed by taking at random any example from the *Amoretti* of Edmund Spenser. (It is, incidentally, peculiar that the influence of Lorenzo's school of versifiers on Spenser's development is seldom recognised although his debt to the earlier Italian poets and the Platonic school is fully acknowledged.)

It almost appears that Lorenzo was conscious of his limitations, since self-deception was not one of his vices. There is, admittedly, a moving commentary on the death of Simonetta which leads to one of his better sonnets with more than a touch of genuine fervour. There is the *Selve d'Amore*, an exercise in amatory verse in that most difficult and constraining of poetic forms, *ottava rima*; and there is the *Corinto*, an agreeable eclogue. More to modern, and possibly to Lorenzo's, taste is *La Caccia col Falcone*, a robust account of a day spent hawking which smells of the very air of Tuscany. But Lorenzo's real achievement as a versifier is to be found in two very difficult poems, *La Nencia da Barberino* and *I Beoni*.

La Nencia, full of bucolic humours and spiced with Tuscan dialect, is an engaging parody of rural life. In this poem Lorenzo comes nearest to a genuine lyric impulse, although admittedly in a low key, and the rhythm is full of life. It is a mark of Lorenzo's extraordinary range that, while his sonnets have some slight resemblance to Spenser's *Amoretti*, the nearest parallel in English to *La Nencia* in its vigour and robust humour is Byron's *Beppo*.

I Beoni, a coarse exercise in *terza rima*, shows all the seaminess which is never far below the Florentine surface. A parody of Dante's *Divina Commedia* written in terms of drunkenness, it is detached and satiric. It explains how Lorenzo could mix with his admirers in the more sinister side streets along the banks of the Arno and still preserve his distance. *I Beoni* confirms Machiavelli's view that Lorenzo found more pleasure in the company of droll and witty men than became a man of his position. For the Medici student, it is a highly revealing work and not the least of the many paradoxes in Lorenzo's career is this Hogarthian picture of low life painted by one who could also write religious poems – the *Lauds* – and, later in life, a sacred play, *S Giovanni e Paolo*.

Despite the growing interest in the native tongue, encouraged by Lorenzo and his court, the classics remained a primary concern of writers throughout the whole of the Medicean age. Florentines would change their own names in the native Tuscan tongue into Latin equivalents; at times even Biblical figures would have their names altered to those of seemingly corresponding Greek deities. It was accordingly no accident that Poliziano first came to notice for his skill as a Latin poet. When Lorenzo looked with favour on his first offering — Book II of the *Iliad* in Latin hexameters — his real career could be said to have started; and it was his ability as a Latin versifier which remained the sure foundation of his fame. He abandoned his ambition of translating the whole of the *Iliad* after the fifth book and, although translations of the Greek epics which have frequently tempted scholars are now not so greatly esteemed as a poetic form, there is no doubt that, from the start, Poliziano showed a great talent for composing musical hexameters. And who could cavil that the *Iliad*, Books II to V, is not in itself a sufficiently formidable achievement?

In both his Latin verse and his prose, Poliziano showed as much originality as the art form allowed. He was no slavish imitator and at times came near to realising one of the great Renaissance aspirations — nothing less than the complete absorption of the works of the ancient classical authors and the adaptation of their essence in a contemporary idiom. As such his work is of great interest to historians, although it is seldom the practice now for classical scholars to enthuse over the Latin writings of anyone later than the Silver Age. The reason for the application of this guillotine in order to deny much of a place to Renaissance and subsequent Latin authors is not always clear, but Poliziano at any rate can claim to rank with many of the best Silver Age authors. Judged by the strictest classical criteria, his main fault was the defect of his genius — an uncontrolled exuberance.

Poliziano's most significant Latin poems, the cantos which comprise the *Sylvae*, were written to serve as prefaces to lectures on the principal classical authors. The *Nutricia*, a comprehensive historical essay on the classical poets, is really his *de arte poetica*. The second canto, the *Rusticus*, provides an informed prologue to the study of Virgil's *Georgics*, but is marred by too much prolixity. The *Manto*, a panegyric on Virgil, has some splendid introductory stanzas, while Homer is celebrated in the *Ambra*. All are marked by profound scholarship and the fluency of the verse.

Before offering examples of Poliziano's Latin poems, a parallel, so far unnoticed, may be mentioned. In the *Nutricia*, Poliziano sets out the classical doctrine of the origin and practice of poetry with inevitable deference to Homer and Virgil. The poem is frequently like Alexander Pope's *Essay on Criticism*. Though the *Essay* owes a great deal to Horace, the tone, the attitude and the general content are strongly reminiscent of the *Nutricia* written some two centuries previously. (We should not be distracted by other similarities between Poliziano and Pope. Poliziano was described as being undersized, bow-legged with a squint, a slightly twisted neck and a large beaked nose. Poor Pope was similarly misshapen. Both depended on the favour of their patrons; both wrote witty and evocative letters. Both remained bachelors and suffered from unrequited love. In Poliziano's case, when he was spurned by Alessandra, the daughter of Chancellor Bartolommeo Scala, in favour of Michael Marullus Tarcagnota, he pursued the unfortunate husband with satiric verse whose vitriol Pope could not have bettered.)

Hear Pope:

> You then whose judgement the right course would steer,
> Know well each ANCIENT'S proper character;
> His Fable, Subject, scope in ev'ry page;
> Religion, Country, genius of his Age:
> Without all these at once before your eyes,
> Cavil you may, but never criticize.
> Be Homer's work your study and delight,
> Read them by day, and meditate by night;
> Thence form your judgment, thence your maxims bring,
> And trace the Muses upward to their spring.
> Still with itself compar'd, his text peruse;
> And let your comment be the Mantuan Muse.
>
> When first young Maro in his boundless mind
> A work t' outlast immortal Rome design'd,
> Perhaps he seem'd above the Critic's law,
> And but from Nature's fountains scorn'd to draw:
> But when t' examine ev'ry part he came,
> Nature and Homer were, he found, the same.
> Convinc'd, amaz'd, he checks the bold design:
> And rules as strict his labour'd verse confine,
> As if the Stagirite o'erlook'd each line.
> Learn hence for ancient rules a just esteem;
> To copy Nature is to copy them.

Poliziano, in the more extravagant diction of the period, has much the same message in the *Nutricia*:

> . . . etenim ut stellas fugere undique caelo,
> Aurea cum radios Hyperionis exeruit fax,

Cernimus, et teneum velut evanescere lunam;
Sic veterum illustres flagranti obscurat honores
Lampade Maeonides: unum quem dia canentem
Facta virum, et saevas aequantem pectine pugnas,
Obstupuit, prorsusque parem confessus Apollo est.
Proximus huic autem, vel ni veneranda senectus
Obstiterit, fortasse prior, canit arma virumque
Vergilius, cui rare sacro, cui gramine pastor
Ascraeus, Siculusque simul cessere volentes.[3]

(In this chapter I have for the most part used the wholly admirable, if sometimes slightly mannered, translations by John Addington Symonds; these translations are to be found in the notes at the end of the chapter.)

Throughout the *Nutricia* Poliziano invokes other classical writers without any great originality of thought or feeling, before turning to the earlier Italian poets, Dante and Petrarch and concluding with a panegyric on Lorenzo. The *Rusticus*, though much less of a loyal catalogue, ends, too, with an address to his patron:

Talia Fesuleo lentus meditabar in antro,
Rure suburbano Medicum, qua mons sacer urbem
Maeoniam, longique volumina despicit Arni:
Qua bonus hospitium felix placidamque quietem
Indulget Laurens, Laurens haud ultima Phoebi
Gloria, jactatis Laurens fida anchora Musis;
Qui si certa magis permiserit otia nobis,
Afflabor majore Deo, nec jam ardue tantum
Silva meas voces, montanaque saxa loquentur,
Sed tu, si qua fides, tu nostrum forsitan olim,
O mea blanda altrix, non aspernabere carmen,
Quamvis magnorum genetrix Florentia vatum,
Doctaque me triplici recinet facundia lingua.[4]

The *Manto* is fully symptomatic of the Renaissance reverence for Virgil. The *Ambra*, the last canto of the *Sylvae*, forms a scholarly study of Homer, and is rounded off with a felicitous reference to the Medici villa at Caiano:

Et nos ergo illi grata pietate dicamus
Hanc de Pierio contextam flore coronam,

Quam mihi Cajanas inter pulcherrima nymphas
Ambra dedit patriae lectam de gramine ripae;
Ambra mei Laurentis amor, quem corniger Umbro,
Umbro senex genuit domino gratissimus Arno,
Umbro suo tandem non erapturus ab alveo.[5]

Fluency of verse, some originality in diction, and an occasional flight of inspiration which overcomes the restrictions imposed by the need to celebrate his patron, these are the main features of Poliziano's Latin poems. In sum they are a substantial achievement, and the *Sylvae* as a whole can claim a respectable place in the history of Latin verse. Less interest is aroused by his fairly pedestrian lyrics (although some merit has been found in the two elegies *In Violas* and *In Lalagen* and the sensitive ode *In Puellam Suam)* and the few Greek elegiacs which have survived. There is also the peculiar satire, which was not published until 1954, called *Sylva in Scabiem* which describes the symptoms of scabies in dreadfully realistic fashion. In all they are enough to justify the epitaph on his tomb in San Marco:

Politianus
in hoc tumulo jacet
Angelus unum
qui caput et linguas
res nova tres habuit.
Obiit an. MCCCCLXXXXIV
Sep. XXIV. Ætatis
XL.[6]

One of Poliziano's earliest compositions in Italian was still written in Classical form and serves as a bridge between his works in Latin and in his native tongue. Poliziano wrote the *Orpheus* during a visit to Mantua in 1471 when he was eighteen years old. (There is an alternative theory that it dates from 1480, but it is clearly a youthful work.) The play was written at the request of Cardinal Gonzaga and was performed to celebrate the visit of Duke Galeazzo Maria Sforza. It was dedicated in a letter to Carlo Canale, the husband of Vanessa who gave birth to Cesare and Lucrezia Borgia:

It was a custom among the Lacedaemonians, my most learned Messer Carlo, when some child of theirs was born either with some maimed members or with strength impaired, to expose him immediately nor to allow him to be kept alive, for they judged such progeny to be unworthy of Lacedaemonia. Thus I also desired that the fable of Orpheus, which I had composed at the request of our most reverend Mantuan cardinal in two days in the midst of continuous disturbances and in vulgar style so that it might be better understood by the spectators, should immediately, not unlike Orpheus, be torn piecemeal, knowing that this little daughter of mine was of the kind to bring her father shame rather than honour and more apt to cause him sorrow than happiness. But seeing that you and some others who love me beyond my deserts maintain her in life against my will, it is indeed fitting that I should have more respect for paternal love and for your wish than for my logical intention. You have, however, a just excuse for your wish; for since my offspring was born under the auspices of so clement a lord, she merits exemption from the general law. Let her, therefore, live, since this is your pleasure; but I protest to you that such kindness is the greatest cruelty, and to this judgement of mine I desire this epistle to be witness. And you, who know the necessity of my obedience and the poverty of the time, I pray you to resist with your authority any one who may attempt to ascribe the imperfection of such a child to the father. Vale.[7]

The defensive, apologetic attitude to the use of Italian is of interest. The *Orpheus*, which is one of the earliest pastoral dramas, was also the first play written in Italian on a non-religious theme. It is an innocent work, more akin perhaps to a medieval English mystery play than to its alleged model, the pastoral work of Theocritus. The graceful songs which are included in the text were apparently sung at Mantua accompanied by musical instruments, so that *Orpheus* has a respectable place in the history of opera.

The tragedy of *Orpheus* tells how a shepherd, Apollo's son Aristaeus, loved Euridice who was married to Orpheus and one day pursued her so ardently as to bring about her death. As she fled from him she was stung by a serpent and fell dead. Orpheus's vocal accomplishments won her back from the underworld, but he disobeyed Pluto's command and turned back to look at her so that she disappeared once more into Hades. Orpheus forswore womankind and aroused the anger of the Maenads who rent him to death.

A modern audience requires to undergo a very deliberate suspension of disbelief in order to take pastoral plays like the *Orpheus* seriously. It may be that our appreciation of early classical and Italian drama is too much coloured by Housman's famous parody of Greek tragedy:

ERI (within): O, I am smitten with a hatchet's jaw;
And that in deed and not in word alone.
CHORUS: I thought I heard a sound within the house
Unlike the voice of one that jumps for joy.
ERI: He splits my skull, not in a friendly way,
Once more: he purposes to kill me dead.
CHORUS: I would not be reputed rash, but yet
I doubt if all be gay within the house.
ERI: O! O! another stroke! that makes the third.
He stabs me to the heart against my wish.
CHORUS: If that be so, thy state of health is poor;
But thine arithmetic is quite correct.

But, even if it is defective in characterisation and lacks any real tragic development, the *Orpheus* contains much to charm its audience. The directness of the opening question by the old shepherd, Mopus, 'Has thou seen my white calf that has a spot of black on its forehead and two red feet and red its knees and flank?' sets the tone. The shepherd, announcing the death of Euridice, does so in admirably limpid language. In Lord's translation:

Orpheus, I bring thee cruel tidings. Thy Nymph so fair is dead. She was fleeing Aristaeus. And when she was come to the brook a serpent, venomous and baneful, which lurked 'neath the grass and the flowers, stung her foot. So potent, so cruel was the hurt that there at once was finished flight and life.

Pluto's astonished response when he hears Orpheus come singing to Hades does, however, contain an element of almost self-conscious parody in the number of classical allusions he manages to pack into two sentences:

Who is he that with so sweet a note and with his glorious lyre moves the abyss? I see Ixion's wheel stand still, Sisyphus sitting on his stone, and the Danaids standing with empty urn. Nor does the water longer shrink from Tantalus, and I behold Cerberus of the triple mouth listening and the Furies grow calm at his command.

But there is much to admire in Orpheus's plea to Pluto:

To thee at last all things return. To thee each mortal life must fall. All that the horned moon beholds must to thy country come. This path each mortal soon or late must tread. Here lies our final goal. Thenceforth thy longer reign awaits us. This my Nymph is destined to thee when so e'er Nature shall grant her her own death. Now with cruel pruning knife thou hast cut the tender vine, and bitter are the grapes. Who is it that mows the grain-field while it is yet green? So give me back my hope.

Throughout Poliziano's Italian poems it is apparent that his inherent poetical ability was at least equal to his learning and scholarship. In him for the first time the urbanity of the classics is fully integrated with the freshness and vigour of the native tongue. From the start his skill in scansion, derived from long study of Latin and Greek authors, can be seen, and he found no trouble in writing light-hearted songs and ballads for the Medici household. They are fluent and their main defect appears to be an occasional delight in form for its own sake. A more serious criticism is the complete lack of any semblance of Roman *gravitas*. Poliziano was a scholar, a wit and a poet, but he was not of a profoundly serious disposition. Such criticism may, however, seem carping and, in any event, is only relevant if Poliziano is to be considered as a candidate for promotion to the very top ranks of poets.

His great poem, the *Stanze per la Giostra,* written to celebrate Giuliano's joust which took place in 1478, shows how completely he had for the first time mastered the use of *ottava rima* and made it into a flexible instrument to express a great range of emotion. But the poem is concerned with a fairly trivial subject; a masked tournament when even the jousting itself was of a fairly spurious character. It is as though T.S. Eliot had concentrated the whole range of his ability to describe the Badminton horse trials.

Such plot as there is in *La Giostra* consists of Giuliano daring to mock at love and prefer hunting where he follows a White Hind, who is meant to represent the beautiful Simonetta. The god of love is not prepared to take this slight without reply; he causes Giuliano to fall in love; and then departs for his own country where, in the second book, any semblance of plot soon disappears. The poem was left unfinished after Giuliano was murdered on 26 April 1478.

Poliziano had, however, found an art form which placed no restriction on the free play of the senses. The attraction of *La Giostra* lies in the sensuous interpretation of nature by one who was steeped in learning but still had a genuine feeling for the Tuscan countryside. The merger of the classics and native fervour, the ubiquitous recipe for success in the Quattrocento, is the basis of Poliziano's poetry.

It is possible to derive a great deal of pleasure from any part of *La Giostra* taken at random — the invocation of the Age of Gold or the account of Ariadne and the Bacchic revels. There is nothing better than the picture of Simonetta as Giuliano finds her in the meadow:

> Candida è ella, e candida la vesta,
> Ma pur di rose e fior dipinta e d' erba;
> Lo inanellato crin dall' aurea testa
> Scende in la fronte umilmente superba.
> Ridegli attorno tutta la foresta,
> E quanto può sue cure disacerba,
> Nell' atto regalmente è mansueta;
> E pur col ciglio le tempeste acqueta.[8]

Nowhere is poetry nearer to the plastic arts than in the Medici spring-time and there is no difficulty in detecting the affinity between Poliziano's poem and the paintings of Botticelli and Gozzoli in particular. The description of Venus rising from the waves is quoted for its connection with Botticelli:

> Vera la schiuma, e vero il mar direste
> Il nicchio ver, vero il soffiar de venti
> La Dea negli occhi folgorar vedreste
> E'l ciel riderle attorno, e gli elementi:
> L'Orepremer l'arena in bianche veste,
> L'aura incrspar li crin distesi e lenti:
> Non una, non diversa esser lor faccia;
> Come par che a sorelle ben confaccia.

> Giurar potresti, che dell'onde uscisse
> La Dea premendo con la destra il crino,
> Con l'altra il dolce pomo ricoprisse:
> E stampata dal piè sacro e divino,
> D'erba e di fior la rena si vestisse:
> Poi con sembiante lieto e pellegrino
> Dalle tre Ninfe in grembe fosse accolta
> E di stellato vestimento involta.[9]

> Real seemed the foam, light floated o'er the sea
> The well dissembled shell by breezes fanned:
> Flashed from the Goddess' eye, a living ray
> Illum'd the smiling heav'n, the main, the land.
> Attendant Hours in snowy vests, display
> Their tresses to the wind, and tread the strand:
> Not one their air — nor varying yet in mien:
> In each fair face a sister's likeness seen.
>
> The Goddess' self (such skill the sculptor's) there
> Emergent moves: from her wet hair the brine
> Her right hand wrings: the left her bosom fair
> Protects: spontaneous green and flowers combine
> Their gayest hues, her earliest steps to share:
> With smiling grace, nor less than forms divine
> Three duteous nymphs receive the stranger blest,
> And with a spangled robe her limbs invest.

Poliziano had, too, the succinctness that comes with full mastery of his medium. See how he improves on the best of Lorenzo — even 'quant' è bella giovenezza' with:

> Sicché, fanciulle, mentre è piu fiorita,
> Cogliam la bella rosa del giardino.

Poliziano's most compelling interest, however, remained in the study and exposition of the classics, although much of his time was spent in composing more trivial verse to meet the wishes of his patrons. The *canzoni, rispetti* and *ballate* written to celebrate the nocturnal jaunts of Lorenzo and his friends are lively and musical and they have Poliziano's unerring sense of style. But the evocation of amatory escapades soon grows cold when the author is not personally committed, and it is so with Poliziano.

Both Poliziano and Marsilio Ficino are sometimes given credit for a share in the work of the third major poet in the Medici circle — Luigi Pulci. Luigi himself was one of three distinguished brothers: Bernardo, the eldest, had translated Virgil's eclogues and written sacred verse; Luca wrote verses on the earlier *giostra* of Lorenzo (a work of more historical than literary merit); but Luigi was much the sharpest of the three. He openly disavowed the influence of the humanists, still popular in Florence, and he combined occasional bouts of piety with a more consistently sceptical outlook. He was the favourite of Lorenzo's mother, Lucrezia, and, perhaps in consequence, it was his wit that aroused Lorenzo's wife, Clarice, to most indignation.

Pulci is remembered for one work: his *Morgante Maggiore* – a farrago which could only have been produced in the Florence of the Quattrocento. It purports to be a vernacular version of the *Chanson de Roland* and is in two parts. The first twenty-three cantos, a satiric account of the adventures of Orlando, Rinaldo and other knights, is followed by five final cantos in more serious vein telling the story of Roncesvalles. But the basic narrative is of secondary importance. The *Morgante* is essentially an urban work. Pulci, encouraged by Lucrezia, produced it, canto by canto, for the delight of Lorenzo and his friends at their banquets in the Medici Palace in the Via Larga. Woven into the ostensibly chivalric story is an endless stream of reflections and comments on topical themes. The verse varies from the serious to the sentimental and from the satiric to the openly ribald. Religious invocations are followed by scepticism and impiety and the whole poem contains much vernacular which is practically untranslatable.

In the midst of the pungent aphorisms which punctuate the verse, three characters are remarkably well realised – Morgante, the jovial glutton; Margutte, a recognisably Rabelaisian figure through whom Pulci pours all his satire on the pretension of scholars and who laughs himself to death; and Astarotte, the devil himself who, with characteristic irony, pronounces Pulci's more apparently profound theological views.

No one has succeeded in translating the *Morgante* and reproducing anything of its original flavour. It is probably an impossible task. The following passage however, describing the slaughtered Christians crowding into heaven, gives something of the poem's flavour:

E cosi in ciel si faceva apparecchio
D' ambrosia e nettar con celeste manna,
E perchè Pietro alla porta è pur vecchio,
Credo che molto quel giorno s' affanna;
E converrà ch' egli abbi buono orecchio,
Tanto gridavan quelle anime Osanna
Ch' eran portate dagli angeli in cielo;
Sicchè la barba gli sudava e 'l pelo.[10]

Notes

1. Guicciardini, *History of Florence,* ed. J.R. Hale (Richard Sadler and Brown Ltd., London, 1966).
2. Ibid.
3. 'As from the heavens we see the stars on all sides fleeing, when the golden torch of the sun-god rises, and the diminished moon appears to fade; so with his burning lamp Maeonides obscures the honours of the earlier bards. Him alone, while he sang the divine deeds of heroes, and with his lyre arrayed fierce wars, Apollo, wonder-struck, confessed his equal. Close at his side, or higher even, but for the veneration due to age, Vergil intones the song of arms and the hero — Vergil, to whom from holy tilth and pasture land both Ascra's and Sicilia's shepherds yield their sway with willing homage.' *Quinque Illustrium Poetarum Carmina,* p. 167.
4. 'On themes like these I spent my hours of leisure in the grottoes of Fiesole, at the Medicean villa, where the holy hill looks down upon the Maeonian city, and surveys the windings of the distant Arno. There good Lorenzo gives his friends a happy home and rest from cares; Lorenzo, not the last of Phoebus' glorious band; Lorenzo, the firm anchor of the Muses tempesttost. If only he but grant me greater ease, the inspiration of a mightier god will raise my soul; nor shall the lofty woods alone and mountain rocks resound my words; but thou — such faith have I — thou too shalt sometimes hear, kind nurse of mind, nor haply scorn my song, thou, Florence, mother of imperial bards, and learned eloquence in three great tongues shall give me fame.' *Carmina,* etc. p. 196.
5. 'We also, therefore, with glad homage dedicate to him this garland twined of Pieria's flowers, which Ambra, loveliest of Cajano's nymphs, gave to me, culled from meadows on her father's shores; Ambra, the love of my Lorenzo, whom Umbrone, the horned stream, begat — Umbrone, dearest to his master Arno, Umbrone, who now henceforth will never break his banks again.' *Carmina,* etc. p. 224.
6. 'Poliziano lies in this grave, the angel who had one head and, what is new, three tongues. He died 24 September 1494, aged 40.'
7. Politian and Tasso, *The Orpheus and Aminta,* translated by L.E. Lord (Oxford University Press, 1931).
8. 'White is the maid, and white the robe around her,
    With buds and roses and thin grasses pied;
    Enwreathed folds of golden tresses crowned her,
    Shadowing her forehead fair with modest pride:
    The wild wood smiled; the thicket, where he found her
    To ease his anguish, bloomed on every side:
    Serene she sits, with gesture queenly mild,
    And with her brow tempers the tempests wild.'
9. W. Parr Gresswell, *Memoirs of Angelus Politianus* etc. (Cadell and Davies, London, 1805).
10. J.A Symonds, *The Renaissance in Italy: The Revival of Learning* (John Murray, London, 1920), p. 393.

8 THE MEDICI ARTISTS (I)

Fifteenth-century Florence saw the fine flowering of the Renaissance in all the arts. The Medici family encouraged the practitioners who came to their court to such effect that the Florentine school dominated the development of the arts in Italy and, as a result, throughout Europe. The problem in describing this fair scene is twofold. First, there is the extraordinary versatility of the Florentine man of arts. Few of them were content to concentrate on a single medium: they were frequently sculptors, architects, painters and writers as well as promoters of original scientific studies. Alberti is a striking instance of a Renaissance scholar who could practise all the arts with skill; but there were many others. Secondly, the very number of the Florentine artists, in the genuine sense, raises its own difficulties and makes selection a daunting task. It becomes necessary, for example, to disregard some able artists who flourished in the Medici period, including Domenico Veneziano, or Filippino Lippi, Botticelli's expert pupil, or Piero de' Cosimo, greatly valued for his strange blend of the real and the unreal.

The fore-runners of the Renaissance fall outside the ambit of a book on the main Medici period, significant though their personal influence was. This is not the place to deal at large with Nicola or Giovanni Pisano or with Cimabue (c. 1240 – c. 1302) who belong to the thirteenth century. It is, however, impossible to pass completely over Cimabue, a controversial figure whose reputation owes much to Dante who puts him in Purgatory because of his pride. Vasari says that Cimabue was of noble Tuscan birth and that while studying at Santa Maria Novella he was attracted by the Greek mural painters who were engaged on decorating the walls. Showing promise, he was eventually apprenticed to the Greeks whom he soon surpassed in form and colour. There is some doubt concerning this version. Santa Maria Novella was not begun until some forty years after Cimabue's death, but it incorporates part of an earlier building, so Vasari's story is possible though improbable. Cimabue's work combines earlier Byzantine influence in his feeling for iconography and hieratic dignity – the old Tuscan wooden crucifix tradition as in the transept at Upper Assisi – and some Roman influence in his structural genius. In general, Cimabue represents the best features of pre-Giotto Tuscan painting. He was also a mosaicist and, shortly before his death, he was working on a mosaic (a figure of St John is extant) in the Pisa Duomo.

No account of Florentine painting, whatever its compass, would be complete without reference to Giotto (1266–1337) who restored the art of design, in Vasari's sense of draughtsmanship or simply drawing.[1] Giotto is the first real personality in Italian painting and much of his work survives together with many anecdotes about his career. He was born at Vespignano, not far from Florence, the son of a peasant farmer called Bondone. The legend is that Cimabue by accident came across Giotto tending his father's sheep and drawing one of them by scratching an image on rock with a pointed stone. Cimabue recognised an unusual native talent and enrolled him as a pupil. One of the two most celebrated stories about Giotto's subsequent career relates how, when a Papal emissary asked the already famous artist for an example of his work to show to His Holiness, Giotto replied by drawing a simple circle on a sheet of paper, confident that the purity of his line would prevail. The second is a tale concerning one of the earlier examples of *trompe l'œil:* Giotto painted on the nose of one of Cimabue's figures a fly so lifelike that Cimabue tried repeatedly to brush it off with his hand.

Giotto remains an enormously significant figure in the history of Western European art. Earlier painting shows scarcely a trace of observation from nature. Giotto's precise observation is seen in his facial expressions, bodily attitudes, and the way in which his drapery conforms to the body – although his trees are still formalised. True observation of nature and, as Berenson has noted, the unusual ability to create tactile impressions to add depth, form the basis of his art. He marks a clean break with the traditional hieratic manner of the Byzantines: his short thick-set figures contrast with the artificial elongation of the Byzantine artists. All his compositions are based on the rectangle, the form best suited to express stability of masses.

Giotto became a wealthy man, unusual in an artist of the time, and was greatly in demand throughout Italy. His virtue is best seen in his undisputed work – the frescoes in the Arena Chapel at Padua and in the church of Santa Croce in Florence. The Arena Chapel is a long aisleless church with a barrel vault. Giotto overcame at once the difficulty – which does not occur in flat Byzantine decoration – caused by his original three-dimensional form of painting. This is done by dividing the walls into unrelated picture spaces which are then treated independently to create the illusion that the paintings are looking through the wall. Giotto uses this method on the two side walls, but on the end wall he relates the entire painting to its setting, adding architectural details to complete the illusion. The whole work provides a singularly satisfying comprehensive form of decoration, and if vices and virtues have to be personified — to our eyes an unimpressive fashion — Giotto makes the most of it.

Two later sets of frescoes are to be found in the chapels of Santa Croce in Florence: the Bardi Chapel with scenes from the life of St Francis, and the Peruzzi Chapel with scenes from St John the Evangelist and St John Baptist. Unfortunately, these frescoes, which had been whitewashed, are now very much restored so that their effect is less impressive. Vasari, however, was greatly touched by the dramatic global tears of the friars lamenting the death of the saint in the Bardi Chapel and, as elsewhere in Giotto, the ease, the vivid nature and the extraordinary proportion of his painting are evident.

Two further examples of Giotto's work may be mentioned as instances of his ubiquitous ability. The *Navicella* mosaic above the three doors of the portico in the courtyard of St Peter's in Rome gives a remarkably lifelike picture of the apostles in their ordeal on the storm-tossed sea and, although this particular mosaic is now in poor repair, Vasari points to the lifelike mixture of apprehension and patience on the faces of the fishermen. Even in this medium the humanism of the Renaissance is foreshadowed. Another work of Giotto's, now more esteemed for its curiosity than its aesthetic value, is the Campanile of Santa Maria del Fiore. Giotto designed the model for this extraordinary tower, 288 feet high, so proportioned that to look out from it induces immediate vertigo, and also planned some of the marble panels which were at least among the first examples of relief work. This was some three years before his death in 1337 and the Campanile was finished by his pupil, Taddeo Gaddi. Giotto was buried in Santa Maria del Fiore. He left an enviable reputation as a painter, an architect, a writer and a wit. Later, by command of Lorenzo the Magnificent, a bust of him was placed in the cathedral along with an apt encomium by Poliziano. But Giotto's lasting fame relies on the influence which he had on his successors.

Lorenzo Ghiberti (1378–1455) was more of a craftsman than an inspired artist, but a craftsman of such meticulous skill that his reputation survives — based principally, for the layman, on a single work, the two doors which he designed for the Baptistery of San Giovanni. In 1401 the Signoria and the Cloth-Makers Guild decided to hold a competition for a second bronze door to match the original one by Andrea Pisano. The competition was generously organised and the seven approved candidates, who included Ghiberti, Brunelleschi and Jacopo della Quercia, were given a year's free residence in Florence while they completed a *Sacrifice of Isaac* relief in the quatrefoil shape of Andrea Pisano's door. There were thirty-four judges, including Giovanni de' Bicci — one of the first overt connections between the Medici and the arts. In his *Commentarii*, a self-laudatory account of his own works, Ghiberti said that the decision was unanimous in his favour, but Brunelleschi claimed that the judges had been rigged.

Ghiberti's qualifications for the task were impressive. He had trained with his father as a goldsmith, he was expert at casting bronzes, and he was gaining fame as a painter at Pesaro when he returned to Florence to embark on the first bronze door which he finished in 1424 — to be followed by a second one that occupied the rest of his working life. Ghiberti's first door follows the same arrangement as Andrea Pisano, with fourteen quatrefoil panels on each side. Twenty panels show the life of Christ from the Annunciation to the Resurrection, while the eight lower panels have single figures of the four Evangelists and the four Doctors of the Church. They show great technical skill in casting, much grace in composition and an almost over-deliberate search for beauty. The head with the turban in the crossborder of the first door is thought to be a self-portrait, and the panels display the first signs of portraiture done from life.

The second door which Ghiberti started in 1425 was meant to follow the same pattern as the first one, but the craftsman felt irked by the restrictions which the old-fashioned quatrefoil imposed. In 1436 he scrapped the work and redesigned it in ten rectangular panels which were all cast by 1447 and assembled by 1452. It was discovered after the last war that the original gilding which had been used on details in the first door and, less effectively, on whole panels on the second, still survived. Ghiberti shows more interest in architectural backgrounds and in perspective in his second door, but he fails to make use of space and his details are too precise. Like Fra Angelico, he is a transitional figure, blending Gothic with the new enthusiasm for the classics. His work was greatly esteemed by his fellow-citizens: he was given a farm near the abbey of Settimo and made a member of the Signoria. Judging by the tone of the *Commentarii* in which he is very pleased with himself, it is easy to visualise how complacently he must have accepted this honour as his just reward.

Filippo Brunelleschi (1377–1446) is the great dominating figure in Renaissance architecture and his style was practised with little variation till the end of the fifteenth century. Brunelleschi was the supreme individualist who, as a result, inspired hostility and affection in equal measure. The main features of his stormy career speak for themselves:

his lifelong rivalry with Ghiberti; his departure along with Donatello for Rome when he lost the competition for the Baptistery door; his enthusiastic study of ancient classical models in the Eternal city (as the Adam Brothers were to do centuries later); his return to Florence and his testy negotiation with the Signoria before he was commissioned to finish Arnolfo di Cambio's dome for the Cathedral of Santa Maria del Fiore; his fury when Ghiberti was appointed as a colleague to assist in supervising the work; his gradual elimination of Ghiberti; and his fluctuating relationship with the Medici family.

Everything he did marked him out as a great figure in the history of architecture. It was probably fortunate that he lost the competition for the Baptistery door since, looking at the model he submitted, he was more likely to prosper as an architect than as a sculptor. His cupola for the dome is his monument more lasting than bronze. Its prestige as the first Renaissance dome was enormous and it had great influence on subsequent ones, including St Peter's in Rome. Even after the Renaissance the steeper-than-hemisphere domes can all be traced back to Brunelleschi. But his achievement was a technical one of construction, derived from his study of the Pantheon at Rome and other ancient models, rather than of innovation. The diameter of the dome is 138 feet and the height from the cornice to the eye of the dome is 133 feet. The form is accordingly almost equilateral: the inner and outer shells are nearly concentric and the secret was that this, combined with the arch form, greatly minimised the thrust at the top of the drum. Nothing more clearly demonstrates the aspiration of the Florentine Renaissance.

Apart from the dome, Brunelleschi's abiding genius can be seen from a few of his exemplary masterpieces, the best known being the Ospedale dei Innocenti, the Basilica of San Lorenzo and the Pazzi Chapel in the cloister of San Marco. The Ospedale (1421–1424) was Brunelleschi's first commission from Giovanni de' Bicci. It has a fine *loggia* and an imposing exterior gracefully apt to its purpose. Brunelleschi was also invited by Cosimo de' Medici to design his new town house, but Cosimo found his plans too ostentatious and gave the commission to Michelozzo. The forthright character of Brunelleschi was likely to lead to a fairly abrasive situation with his Medici patron, but he was also given the task of designing much of the rebuilding of the family church of San Lorenzo. The Old Sacristy, the transept and the choir were mostly completed to his design during his lifetime. There is much to be said for the simple harmony of proportion with very little ornament, but to modern eyes San Lorenzo lacks any compelling aesthetic appeal.

Despite his intermittent relationship with the Medici, Brunelleschi's most graceful work was done for the rival Pazzi family. Many consider the Pazzi chapel to be the most elegant building in Florence. The exterior with its coffered Roman barrel vault carried on six Corinthian columns is an entirely new form of composition using classical elements but without imitating the facade of a Roman temple. The interior surface is a masterly contrast of white plaster with dark stone outlining the architectural forms, and the whole tone is one of lightness, delicacy and elegance.

Brunelleschi's excellences defy any attempt to itemise them. He had, as much as any of the Medici court, a profound knowledge of classical architecture, but he used the antique, he never copied it. Such was the sincerity of his style that he would not hide architectural faults under profuse ornament. His austerity was at times too severe but he had a consistent feeling for proportion and spatial arrangement. In him — as was the case with Poliziano in another field — the inspiration of the classics was truly fused in the spirit of the Renaissance, and all fifteenth-century architects worked under his shadow.

Michelozzo (1396–1472) was one architect whose agreeable talent was inevitably overshadowed by the achievements of Brunelleschi from whom he derived many of his ideas. Primarily a craftsman, he first appears along with Ghiberti helping with work on the first door, and for some time he was employed as a diecutter in the Florentine mint. He did, however, benefit greatly from his friendship with the Medici and he accompanied Cosimo into his brief period of exile in Venice in 1434–36. Soon after his return, Cosimo employed him to reconstruct the cloister of San Marco. This proved a felicitous commission and, while it shows no great innovation, Michelozzo's work blends well with the frescoes of Fra Angelico. In 1444 he began the Medici Palace after Cosimo had discarded Brunelleschi's design. In retrospect, however, Michelozzo's design shows many traces of Brunelleschi's influence. It is a typical Florentine building with a wisely strong construction of the walls on the ground floor in the rough texture known as *rustica* and a heavy top cornice. Another Medici commission was the family bank at Milan, while the rest of his working career was mainly spent on the redecoration of the interior of the Palazzo Vecchio. Michelozzo's significance is to show how much contemporary architects relied on Brunelleschi for inspiration and on the Medici family for support.

Just as Brunelleschi dominates all fifteenth-century architects, so

Donatello (1386–1466) is the leading figure in Florentine sculpture. His productivity was immense and, by his absorption of classical influences into his own individual style, he provided an inspiring model for his contemporaries and successors. Donatello was a close friend of Cosimo de' Medici and, after Cosimo's death, his son Piero gave him a farm and eventually a pension for his old age. There is evidence that it was Donatello who persuaded Cosimo to start his great collection of antiques. For Cosimo, too, he did the elegant roundels to decorate the *cortile* of the Palazzo Medici, and the bronze David which marks an important stage in his development.

Much can be learned of Donatello's growing power from a comparison of his two *David* portrayals. The earlier marble one in the Bargello, done between 1410 and 1412, already shows his vitality (the large, coarse hands are typical of Donatello) but it is clearly a development from fourteenth-century Gothic with its mannered display. The later bronze *David*, executed at least twenty years later, shows how Donatello had been influenced by humanism in the interval. Greatly praised for its technical competence, it now depicts an individual human body rather than a Gothic transcendental type.

The extraordinary range of Donatello's work shows Renaissance man at his best, making use of classical models — though few antiquities were then available apart from the ruins which he had seen in Rome — to mould a new humanist concept, an interest in everything that affected mankind. It is clear that Cosimo recognised Donatello's powerful genius and found his ideas compatible with his own. In the absence of a lengthy catalogue, Donatello's permanent contribution to Renaissance art can be seen in his use of the technique of low relief, a sophisticated, restrained medium which he developed best in the *Ascension and Keys of St Peter* (now in the Victoria and Albert Museum); the technical representation of crowds as in the relief at the Campo Santo in Padua, and the *Dance of Salome* relief (at Lille) which shows an unusually clear perspective; the nude free-standing statue of which the bronze *David* in the Bargello is a supreme example; the group statue of the same genre — the *Judith and Holofernes* done for the Signoria, which so satisfied Donatello that, for the first time, he signed his work with the rubric 'Donatello Opus'; and the equestrian statue like that of *St George* in armour which shows at once youth, courage and knightly valour. Happy throughout his life, and a less prickly character than Brunelleschi, Donatello is the splendid example of a Medici protégé.

Luca della Robbia (1400–82) did his best work as a sculptor — the

Cantoria in the Duomo — early in his career and thereafter he was best known for the terracotta process which he invented. The Cantoria is a remarkable piece of sculpture. It was designed to illustrate one of the Psalms and shows seventy-four separate figures praising the Lord. The best reliefs are at either end where the composition leads the eye to the front of the gallery. There is a Greek purity of line and an elegance of style which defies definition. The Cantoria had a great deal of influence on contemporary sculptors but Luca was not himself to equal it.

His fame rests chiefly on his method of using tin-glazing. This is a transparent lead-glaze which becomes white when tin is added. It was already familiar in Italian majolica ware, and Luca's innovation was to apply it to baked terracotta. The baked model was dipped in the white glaze; then the coloured parts were wiped clean and coloured glazes applied to them. The whole was then fixed and the colours appeared afterwards. It is very difficult to lay these glazes evenly and Luca's own work is distinguished from his followers by the extraordinary cleanness of his colour and the level surface of the glaze which shows all the subtlety of modelling beneath. His medallion in the Pazzi Chapel admirably complements Brunelleschi's design and the effect is to produce a highly attractive scheme of decoration. From what is known of his character and from what remains of his work, Luca seems detached from the Medici scene. He was more concerned with the terracotta factory which he founded and which remained in his family till about 1530.

Among painters we find in Masaccio the true native genius of the Renaissance, an artist with an inspiration that had been lacking among Florentine painters since Giotto in the previous century. In Berenson's words 'In a career of but a few years he gave to Florentine painting the direction it pursued to the end.' This is a bold claim but it is fully justified. Technically, Masaccio brought to his painting a much fuller understanding of perspective, especially serial perspective, and this was the positive advance of the period. Masaccio's successor, Uccello, showed how perspective could take charge of an artist's work to such an extent that it actually impairs the aesthetic effect. Brunelleschi in all probability worked out the original scientific system of vanishing-point perspective, but Masaccio was the first to apply it to painting. He had also a keen appreciation of the differences of planes in a composition and a strong feeling for the composition as a whole. His style was simple and his colours gay and atmospheric. He was both a realist and an idealist and he made the emotions of his subjects fully apparent.

In more mundane terms, Vasari says that he excelled in foreshortening and was the first to plant feet firmly on the ground as opposed to the practice hitherto of rearing figures precariously on the points of their toes.

When Cosimo de' Medici returned from exile in 1434 — always a crucial date in Florentine history — Masaccio was commissioned to decorate the Brancacci Chapel in the Church of Santa Maria del Carmine. Masolino, the first to undertake this work, had died, and the chapel was finished by Filippino Lippi after the death of Masaccio. There is still some academic dispute about the identity of the artists who painted the individual frescoes, but most of those attributed to Masaccio are clearly his — for example, that showing the *Expulsion from Paradise* where the agony of Adam and Eve is almost vocal. It is no wonder that subsequent Florentine painters made the Brancacci frescoes their first study.

Vasari refers to considerable activity by Masaccio as a portrait painter 'from the life', but unfortunately only his portrait of Giovanni de' Bicci survives. Masaccio's last great work was the Trinity fresco in Santa Maria Novella where the very elaborate perspective is brilliantly executed. The two kneeling figures are said to be those of the commissioners of the fresco, an early Florentine inclusion of donors. In any event, the impressive portraits are obviously drawn from life. Masaccio's followers were to show how much they had learned from him.

Notes

1.   Vasari, *The Lives of the Artists* (Penguin Classics, 1965).

9 THE MEDICI ARTISTS (II)

The main preceptors of the Florentine school, the models to be followed, consciously or unconsciously, were Donatello in sculpture, Brunelleschi as an architect and Masaccio in painting. It was the happy lot of their followers to enjoy both their example and the same social conditions to develop their own genius during the succeeding decades until the expulsion of the Medici in 1492.

The Florentine economy was now sufficiently affluent to ensure the conditions in which the company of artists would flourish. Trade was prosperous; banking activities were well established; there was a growing urban population; and the ruling families cultivated pageantry and all forms of entertainment to the point of extravagance. In the Middle Ages society had been graded and immutable. In the words of Shakespeare's Ulysses 'Take but degree away, untune that string, and, hark, what discord follows!' But many medieval inhibitions had now disappeared. A spirit of curiosity about all aspects of man's activities was abroad. Individual experience was given a new significance; the raw material for all forms of artistic expression was readily available.

A firm base for the new prosperity and the flowering of artistic endeavour was provided by the twenty-one guilds of craftsmen. They comprised only some three or four thousand members, but their influence was immense, both economically and as a source from which many of the leading artists were recruited. The artists came from, or were often apprenticed to, craftsmen for their initial training. For patronage and employment they relied on the wealthy families, and in particular the Medici. Cosimo spent enormous sums on works of sculpture and architecture. Lorenzo worthily maintained the tradition, although his own bent was a more literary one. But throughout the century, until the fall in trade coincided with the end of the first Medici period, many successful Florentines commissioned works of art. They did so as a seeming act of piety, by decorating and embellishing the interiors of churches and chapels. They rejoiced, too, in adorning their own palaces and villas with paintings, frescoes and tapestries. And, as the century proceeded, they increasingly sought their own immortality in portraits drawn from life.

All these conditions, based on a high degree of economic prosperity, combined to create circumstances which, despite the wars and stories

113

of wars that were never far away, could scarcely have been more propitious for the development of the arts. Donatello and Masaccio had already made great advances in technique. The other main achievements of the Florentine school were to follow: a greater feeling for, and a more accurate delineation of, landscape; growing confidence in the use of perspective; a clear appreciation of light and shade; and a fuller appreciation of the nude.

One of Masaccio's most delightful successors was Fra Angelico (1387–1455) who, though older, outlived him by nearly thirty years. Fra Angelico can be distinguished from the company of Florentine painters as that unusual creature of the time, a singularly happy, devout Christian. The utter simplicity and sincerity of his belief is evident both in his religious figures and in his landscapes. No one has conveyed more successfully his delight in being on God's earth or his genuine feeling for nature – as, for example, in the beautiful Tuscan landscape which appears in his *Deposition* fresco now in San Marco Museum. Nor is it any accident that he should have painted the first identifiable Italian landscape (Lake Trasimene).

Originally trained as an illuminator – and his early work accordingly shows a miniature-like technique – he entered the monastery at Fiesole in 1407. For the next thirty years he accompanied his fellow monks to Cortona and Foligno before returning to Fiesole and then to the convent of San Marco. From 1436 until his death in 1455 most of his time was spent in Florence or Fiesole, with an interval of five years in Rome. Throughout his whole career he sought no office or preferment. He is said to have declined the Archbishopric of Florence, but he seems at one stage to have been Prior of Fiesole. He was supremely content to serve his monastic order and to glorify God through his paintings.

Cosimo de' Medici showed more than his usual perception when he asked him to decorate the reconstructed San Marco. For once some worldly topical interest is apparent, caused by the presence in Florence of the many dramatic figures who attended the Council of Churches in 1439. The Council saw frequent processions of the Pope, the Emperor, the Patriarch, prelates and priests in exotic dress. The San Marco fresco of the *Adoration of the Magi* reflects this in the suites of the three Kings, the Eastern headdresses and the Oriental-type faces.

Fra Angelico blends Gothic and Renaissance elements in unusually close fusion. His draperies have a sinuous Gothic line and Gothic ornamentation. His frequent use of pure brilliant colour and gold backgrounds recalls medieval manuscript illumination. But his strong draughtsmanship and the sense of perspective are all

Renaissance, as are his structural settings. His best-known fresco, the *Annunciation* in San Marco, shows a feeling for space, light and luminosity which is essentially contemporary. The whole effect has a strange other-world quality which emphasises Fra Angelico's place as the Christian visionary of the Medici court. He was also capable of work on a larger scale, and Tancred Borenius claims that the St Stephen series of frescoes in the Vatican is his nearest approach to the fully-developed Quattrocento manner. The lofty epic spirit, the breadth of design and the incisiveness of the individual characters are all admirable.

There is certainly nothing sublime or visionary about Fra Angelico's contemporary, Fra Filippo Lippi (1406–69). This preposterous character was obsessed with the demands of the flesh and lived in an extravagant manner not obviously well-suited to the Monastic order which he affected through most of his life. He even succeeded in seducing a beautiful nun, Lucrezia Buti, and extracting her from the Carmelite convent at Prato. But his lust for life, which enlivens his attractive, essentially good-humoured paintings, also made him a popular figure: at least he inspired much affection among the Medici. In 1437 he wrote to Piero de' Medici complaining of his poverty and thereafter he was a recognised Medici artist. Cosimo gave him frequent commissions and tried, ineffectually, to lock him up so that he might finish a fresco without amorous interruption. Filippo died while working at Spoleto and was buried there. He was held in such esteem by the Medici that Lorenzo made a personal expedition to the town seeking the return of his body for interment in Florence. But Spoleto would have none of it: the citizens saw the greatness of the man and determined to retain his tomb in their midst.

Two examples will suffice to illustrate his genius. His earliest certain work, the *Madonna* now in the Tarquinia Museum, shows how he is developing from Masaccio's solid monumental style with his own mannerisms. He is a very mannered painter and there are some strange effects, such as the dark red colour of the flesh in this painting. The better-known *Madonna, Child and Angels*, in the Uffizi, shows the face of the Madonna with characteristically pinched features and angular-cut eyes (not unlike Botticelli's work) and a beautiful romantic landscape with strange rocks imposed to produce a startling effect. Filippo was quite prepared to disregard perspective when it suited him and to concentrate on developing his own poetic moods by wilful distortions. He was not an innovator and his art is naturally lyrical. He had great sensuous gracefulness and charm which expressed his joy in life and all the pleasures, fleshly rather than spiritual, which he saw in the

Florentine scene. Possibly the illustrator of a mood rather than a profound creator, his colouring is usually original and always fascinating.

During the central part of the Medici period, the genial, cultured figure of Leon Battista Alberti (1404–72) exercised a great deal of influence over his fellow architects and artists. None of his own paintings have survived and, while some of his architectural work, such as the Palazzo Rucellai, is important for its intellectual approach, his real significance lies in his theories and his writing. A trained lawyer, a recognised man of letters, one of the first organists, and an accomplished mathematician, he wrote a treatise on architecture in ten volumes, which was one of Lorenzo de' Medici's favourite studies, a further work on painting, and one on education and marriage. Alberti demonstrated in full measure the versatility and energy of the Florentine artist, but he was very much of his time and his interest today is largely historical.

Another artist of indomitable energy who practised as a painter, sculptor and architect was Andrea del Verrocchio (1435–88). He excelled as a craftsman rather than as an imaginative artist, and significantly he was trained as a goldsmith. As a painter he is usually associated with his contemporaries, the Pollaiuolo brothers, particularly Antonio. Most of Verrocchio's painting which has survived is either unfinished or of doubtful authenticity. He seems, however, to have had a feeling for landscape and for the movement of his figures – although he has nothing to rival the lifelike activity in Pollaiuolo's *Battle of the Nudes* in the Uffizi, or *The Martyrdom of Saint Sebastian* in the National Gallery, London. In the latter painting the sense of movement is so intense that it is almost possible to hear the tautening of the crossbows.

Most of Verrocchio's best work was done for the Medici family. For them he designed the tombs of Cosimo in 1467 and that of Piero and Giovanni in 1472 which has some excellent ornamental detail in a restrained manner. (The Medici were by now ostentatiously unostentatious.) The bronze *David* in the Bargello shows how great had been the departure from the virile, heroic figure done by Donatello. Verrocchio's *David* is much more delicate, almost feminine. One inspired statue commissioned by the Medici is the *Cherub with the Dolphin*, now in the courtyard of the Palazzo Vecchio. Lively, delicate and fully expressive of movement in its effect, it is reminiscent of the famous *Jockey* in the National Museum at Athens. The dangers inherent in Verrocchio's approach can, however, be detected in the equestrian statue of the *condottiore*, Bartolommeo Colleoni, in Venice on which he was working when he died. This is a romantic and emotional work: it shows obvious traits of one of the main Italian defects, an ineradicable tendency to overdramatise, to settle for the theatrical solution. The Venetians were pleased with themselves, but so, possibly, was Verrocchio.

Two lesser painters who were more highly esteemed in their day than they are now, but who are still significant in any account of Florentine painting, are Benozzo Gozzoli (1420–97) and Domenico Ghirlandaio (1449–94). Gozzoli first appears in 1444 working with Ghiberti on the second Baptistery door. He also studied for a time with Fra Angelico, but his work of highest virtuosity is his fresco decoration of the chapel in the Palazzo Medici. The whole wall is treated as a tapestry: the conception is entirely decorative and there is no attempt at illusion. Contemporary figures were reproduced but Gozzoli's skill – really as an illustrator – does not seems to have appealed to the Medici who, with unusual tartness, declined to give poor Benozzo any further commissions. The shortcomings in his style – a peculiar, uninspired flatness which is not entirely relieved by his attractive colouring – are particularly obvious in his series of frescoes at the Campo Santo in Pisa. Gozzoli demonstrates that craftsmanship is not enough, and he was not touched by the warm genius found with surprising frequency in the rest of the Medici circle.

Ghirlandaio is remembered as Michelangelo's first teacher. Although he practised in the second half of the century, his work represents the more old-fashioned traditions of the earlier half. His *Last Supper* in the Refectory of the Ognissanti is characteristic of the Florentine *Last Suppers* which appear so often in refectories during this period. His frescoes in the Sassetti Chapel in Santa Trinita are notable for including one of the best likenesses of Lorenzo. In his paintings in the choir of Santa Maria Novella he included some interesting portraits of the Tornabuoni family, and of the famous beauty Ginevra de Benci. But beautiful though these women are, they are frequently lifeless. Ghirlandaio found male figures more congenial. The portrait of the man with the bizarre nose (and his grandson) now in the Louvre shows Ghirlandaio at his most felicitous. The painting is both charming and objective; there is no cruelty and no sentimentality. Throughout much of his painting Ghirlandaio shows a singularly tender realism but he lacked any strong inspiration.

There is no doubt that the spark of genius, the light that never was on sea or land, appears at an early stage in the work of Alessandro Filipepi (1444–1510), commonly called Botticelli, either after the goldsmith with whom he served his apprenticeship or after his eldest brother, Giovanni, who was called Botticello, or 'Little Barrel'. He is sometimes thought to have been the closest to the Medici of all the Florentine painters. His association with them was intimate and lasting. He painted no portrait of Lorenzo but there is at least one of Giuliano and one of Lorenzo's son Piero. In his *Adoration of the Magi*, painted for Santa Maria Novella — a romantic work already showing signs of Botticelli's tendency to escapism — he depicted Cosimo, Giuliano and Cosimo's son, Giovanni, as the three Kings. The *Primavera*, however, was commissioned not, as might have been expected, by Lorenzo the Magnificent, but by a member of the cadet branch of the family, Lorenzo di Pierfrancesco de' Medici, and it was this Lorenzo who kept him in work until his eventual conversion to Savonarola's austere doctrines.

In his early work he is clearly a disciple of Fra Filippo. He often paints the garlands and white and red roses which Filippo admired. He also shows much of his teacher's straightforward solidity in the fresco of *St Augustine* (Uffizi) which he painted for the Vespucci family. This is a serious, traditional study, and the way in which Botticelli eventually cast off the restraints of orthodox representation can be seen by comparing the *St Augustine* with the head of the Centaur in a much later work, *Pallas the Centaur* (Uffizi), painted as an allegory to celebrate Lorenzo's successful termination of the civil war following the Pazzi conspiracy. In the second work the line of the draughtsmanship acquires a new significance and is able by itself to convey the artist's intention. Pure line had not before been used to such abstract effect.

Another work of the late 1470s, *Judith with the Head of Holofernes* (Uffizi) also shows Botticelli's graceful figures in a very mannered fashion. Botticelli is really a mannerist, as is much of the art of this period. But though he painted many allegorical and religious works, including some frescoes for the Sistine Chapel, where his pagan style does not always harmonise with devotional subjects, it is on the *Primavera* and the *Birth of Venus*, both in the Uffizi, that Botticelli's individual reputation rests.

Loosely based on Poliziano's *Stanze*, they were inspired by an idealised, posthumous recollection of the beautiful Simonetta Vespucci. The same sensuous, unworldly vision as is described by Poliziano animates Botticelli's paintings, and the ethereal impression which Simonetta made on her time is fittingly perpetuated. The rhythmic virtues of the two paintings — for example, the inspired architectural use of the natural background of trees to add depth to the evanescent lines of the *Primavera*, and the delicate arrangement of the tresses of hair in the much later *Birth of Venus* — have been often remarked. Traditionally, Simonetta is not the central figure in either painting. She is supposed to be the third figure from the right in the *Primavera* and the figure on the right of Venus in the *Birth*. Botticelli's lyrical lines have little in common with the possibly more realistic portrait of Simonetta by Ghirlandaio in the Ognissanti, where she was buried. But what matters in these paintings, probably the best-known in the whole Uffizi, is the delicate but sweeping use of line to indicate a mood, not for purely representational purposes.

Here is the culmination of the Florentine art of this period. It is lyrical and unmistakably individualistic. Botticelli can, in fact, be regarded as so much of an individualist as to have little importance historically, but he is also acutely affected by the continuing Renaissance dilemma — the conflict between classical humanism, becoming pure hedonism, and the strictures of the Church. As a footnote to Botticelli, Eric Linklater has described how, during the Second World War, he found these two paintings in a Tuscan villa where they had been sent for safe custody. The paintings, guarded unknowingly by the Mahratta Light Infantry who had occupied the villa, were stacked with their faces to the wall. Linklater turned them round and, astounded at his discovery, he knelt and kissed the pregnant Venus, overcome with humility and wonder.

No chapter on the Florentine artists can omit a reference to Leonardo da Vinci (1452–1519) and Michelangelo (1475–1564), who absorbed all the achievements of their Florentine forbears and moulded them in their own image. But they do not, strictly speaking, fall within the scope of this book. Michelangelo, who studied first under Ghirlandaio and came under Lorenzo's patronage for some three to four years, was only seventeen when the latter died in 1492. His great achievements, his perfection of the study of the human nude, were to come later. In any event Michelangelo, though he must have learned from the propinquity of Pico, Poliziano and other Platonists who formed Lorenzo's circle, was more than any other artist a man on his own. His conception, his emotional and religious preoccupations, were too immense in scale for Lorenzo's court.

Much the same is true of Leonardo. Lorenzo has sometimes been accused of neglecting Leonardo's genius but he did in fact support him with commissions in his early career and when Leonardo went to Milan in 1482 it was with a strong recommendation in his favour from

Lorenzo. An early pupil of Verrocchio, Leonardo is the one Florentine unaffected by the classical interests of the Medici adherents. The study of nature in depth and detail was his main artistic commitment, but one that had to compete with his interest in such diverse fields as experimental science, engineering and hydrology. For once, 'Protean' can be safely invoked to describe one who touched nothing that he did not adorn. His main creative period (1483–99) in Milan was spent under the patronage of his friend Ludovico Sforza (il Moro) and it was there that he painted both the supremely graceful *Virgin of the Rocks*, now in the Louvre, and the *Last Supper* in Santa Maria delle Grazie. During one of the periods when he returned to Florence (1503–6), however, he painted the celebrated portrait of Madonna Lisa, the wife of Zanobi del Giocondo. No short summary can do justice to Leonardo's skill in both art and science. In painting he concentrated on light and shade: he seemed to have all the skills of the earlier Florentines, but he absorbed them and made them better. If the supreme product of the Renaissance was an individual whose hallmark was ubiquitous intellectual authority, that man was Leonardo.

10 GIROLAMO SAVONAROLA

Savonarola adds a new dimension to the Medici tapestry. He appears in many different guises: as an ascetic greatly concerned with the problems of the flesh; as an orator and preacher who could rouse his audience to mass hysteria; as a devoted, if not profound, theological scholar; as a prophet with an uncanny capacity for seeming to make his prophecies come true; and as a religious reformer. Nowadays he is not held in great esteem for any of these. His significance is largely historical but nonetheless of continuing interest. He stands out in stark relief against the worldliness of the Florentines and the corrupt practices of the Church. Compared with what seemed to him the futile frivolity of Lorenzo's court he appears as the skeleton at the feast.

During the fifteenth century the affairs of the Holy See and Italian politics were even more than usually inextricable. The Pope was not only a spiritual power; and few fifteenth-century Popes can have expected much spiritual reward for their temporal activities. The greedy determination of Pope Sixtus to found a dynasty and provide for his equally unattractive nephews had already embroiled Italy in a bitter and exhausting conflict. Profligacy reached new depths in the person of Pope Alexander, and subsequent Popes offered little improvement. Savonarola occupies an odd position as a churchman who was interested in politics for purposes of religious reform. But he suffered, eventually, the fate of all puritan zealots. During the period, and only during the period, when his puritan doctrine could be linked with successful political activity, he prevailed. But as soon as the political situation changed, his contemporaries' interest in a continuing piety rapidly withered away. In the England of the Stuarts, puritanism, for long latent, made no progress until it became identified with Parliamentary opposition to Charles I. Savonarola reached the height of his power when the Florentines saw in him their bulwark against the attempts of the Holy See to restore the Medici after their expulsion in 1494. Puritanism in England was soon dissipated when the iniquities of the Stuarts were no longer a threat; Savonarola's influence declined from the time when he ceased to be regarded as the protector of the Florentine Republic.

Savonarola also exemplifies the great conflict of the fifteenth century between the imitation of the classics, prevalent from Petrarch onwards, in thought, taste and the arts, and Catholic Christianity which still attracted adherence, though sometimes only nominally. Although the thinkers of the fifteenth century had in many cases lost the inspiration of Christian faith, they failed to emulate either Greek self-discipline and sense of form or Roman patriotism. To Savonarola's mind it was clear that his contemporaries were worshipping at the shrine of two false gods, the classics and a new conception of style.

Although the struggle between classical paganism and Christianity reached its climax in Savonarola, the elements of contradiction had long been apparent. They start with the essentially individual and pragmatic nature of fifteenth-century Italy. Italy throughout the century, and for long after, was incapable of any coherent system of government. The City States were autonomous; and they were intensely competitive both with each other and within themselves. In this tense atmosphere personal ability and individual talent were more important than birth or inheritance. The legal distinction between the *grandi* and the *popolani* in Florence was eventually of a very surface nature. The achievements of the century were almost entirely individual in character. The great architectural works, like Brunelleschi's Dome, derived from the inspiration of one man, unlike the co-operation which produced the triumphs of Gothic architecture. The Florentine painters, too, were supreme individualists.

The next characteristic which can be identified is the surprising physical force which the Italians frequently manifested to equal the individuality of their approach. Shortly after the end of the century, Castiglione said that the perfect gentleman would be a dancer, rider, wrestler, runner, archer, javelin and quoit thrower, and tennis and *pallone* player. This is a formidable list which would exhaust any twentieth-century athlete.

There seems little doubt that, under Popes who lacked any burning Christian inspiration, the Italians' freedom of thought, inspired as it was by the rediscovery of the classics and the enormous release of physical energy, eventually turned to licentiousness. The conflict between the fifteenth century and the ancient world, in short, promoted a Godless and irreligious mode of life. Petronius was preferred to St Paul and Athens to Jerusalem. Cosimo de' Medici made the same point in more temperate terms: 'You follow infinite objects; I follow the finite; you place your ladders in the heavens, I on earth, that I may not seek so high or fall so low.'[1] Savonarola's beliefs were of a different order.

Girolamo Savonarola was born at Ferrara on 21 September 1452. He was the third of seven children and his two elder brothers in time became, respectively, a soldier and the manager of the family estate. Girolamo was moderately precocious and it was hoped that he would pursue his studies and become a physician like his grandfather, Michael. Unfortunately his grandfather died in 1462 and there was no one left to guide the young Savonarola in his studies. He was not the kind of schoolboy to inspire affection among his classmates. For a time he seems to have lacked any great sense of direction. But this was soon remedied and he subsequently said that from an early age he was inspired by the writings of St Thomas Aquinas which, even during that period, would normally be regarded as doubtfully suitable literature for someone who had not yet reached his teens. Girolamo can scarcely have been an attractive child and his writings reveal that, from an early age, he was of a melancholy and disconsolate nature. With all the impatient arrogance of youth he found little to please him in the extravagant frivolity of the Italian rulers and he had a singularly irresponsible example near home at Ferrara where the rule of Borso d'Este was as purposeless as that of any Italian despot. When he was aged twenty, Girolamo was inspired for once by a more worldly passion for Laodamia Strozzi, the daughter of one of his neighbours, a member of the family who had been exiled from Florence. But Savonarola's advances met with no success and it takes no great perception to see that his subsequent attacks on all fleshly pursuits may well have dated from this event. It was not to be repeated.

Savonarola's thoughts were turning increasingly towards a religious vocation and, on a visit to the town of Faenza, a sermon preached by an Augustine monk led him to decide to contemplate a monastic vocation. A year later he entered the Dominican Convent at Bologna and wrote to his father, in terms somewhat lacking in filial affection and all too like his subsequent lucubrations: 'I could no longer endure the gross corruption of the age, and witness throughout Italy vice triumphant and virtue in the dust.'[2]

For the next seven years Savonarola continued in the most determined way to demonstrate his aggressive religious devotion. Never very robust, he became emaciated by continuing fasts and abstinence and flitted through the cloisters like a spectre, seldom conversing with his fellow monks. Any rewards which he received for this prolonged self-abnegation must have been of a spiritual nature since there is little evidence that his colleagues were sufficiently impressed by his prayers and privations to seek to emulate them.

There is no doubt, however, that at this particular time it was easy for Savonarola to contrast the austerity of monastic life with the corruption of the church in the Holy See under Pope Sixtus and with the general laxity of standards in the main Italian City States. It appeared, for example, that in Naples under Ferdinand, in Venice under Pasquale Malpiero, in Florence under Lorenzo and even in Milan under Galeazzo, the first signs of the permissive society had appeared. The inhibitions preached by the clergy (though not always practised by them) had at least for a time ceased to have much effect. It was also true that the rulers of these four States had all succeeded to power in periods of comparative peace and had not been previously hardened by the sharp competition of internecine wars. It may have been the lack of any political inspiration on the part of the rulers that led to the coincidence of three domestic rebellions in one year, 1476, at Genoa, Ferrara and Florence.

In 1482 Savonarola left Bologna and for a time preached in his native Ferrara without arousing any great interest. From there he went to Florence where he went straight to the Convent of San Marco. It is odd that someone whose whole creed depended on the extremes of austerity should have found his way to one of the most elegant of religious establishments. The Convent itself had been built by Michelozzo to the orders of Cosimo, and subsequently the great library belonging to Niccolo de' Niccoli was housed in it. Niccolo had earlier bankrupted himself by his enthusiasm for acquiring books and depended heavily on help from Cosimo. When he died in 1437 he left his manuscripts to a number of trustees, including Cosimo who paid his debts in exchange for the right to assign the library. Most of Niccolo's manuscripts were placed in the Convent, which has claims to be recognised as the first public library established in Italy.

Niccolo is such an engaging character that he deserves more than a passing mention. He stimulated scholarship by lending the books he had collected, but he was not interested in mere acquisition; he was a student and collator, and he was generous in making his knowledge of antiquity available to young scholars. Vespasiano, in his Life of Niccoli, brings him to life in a passage which will bear quotation again:

> First of all, he was of a most fair presence; lively, for a smile was ever on his lips; and very pleasant in his talk. He wore clothes of the fairest crimson cloth, down to the ground. He never married, in order that he might not be impeded in his studies. A housekeeper provided for his daily needs. He was above all men the most cleanly in eating, as also in all other things. When he sat at table, he ate from fair antique vases; and, in like manner, all his table was covered with

porcelain and other vessels of great beauty. The cup from which he drank was of crystal or of some other precious stone. To see him at table — a perfect model of the men of old — was of a truth a charming sight. He always willed that the napkins set before him should be of the whitest, as well as all the linen. Some might wonder at the many vases he possessed, to whom I answer that things of that sort were neither so highly valued then, nor so much regarded, as they have since become; and Niccolo having friends everywhere, anyone who wished to do him a pleasure would send him marble statues, or antique vases, carvings, inscriptions, pictures from the hands of distinguished masters, and mosaic tablets. He had a most beautiful map, on which all the parts and cities of the world were marked; others of Italy and Spain, all painted. Florence could not show a house more full of ornaments than his, or one that had in it a greater number of graceful objects; so that all who went there found innumerable things of worth to please varieties of taste.

The Convent not only boasted one of the most distinguished Florentine architects; its walls were also decorated with paintings by Fra Angelico. It was in this unlikely location that the zealous friar made his home.

Savonarola did not find the theological and philosophical climate in Florence much to his liking. The enthusiasm for Platonism, which dated from the presence of so many Platonic scholars at the Council of Florence in 1439, was still prevalent. The influence of Gemistos Plethon was still remarkably powerful. Gemistos had spent only three years in Italy, from 1438 to 1441, and had returned to Mistra to die nine years later. Such was his reputation, however, that his body was exhumed by Sigismondo Malatesta and buried at Rimini. Gemistos cannot be regarded as a very satisfactory scholar, and it is surprising that his influence lasted so long. His doctrine consisted of an absurd mixture of neo-Platonism and Greek mythology, linked together by speciously logical arguments.

The real apostle of Platonism in Florence was by now Marsilio Ficino, the son of Cosimo's physician. Marsilio who was born at Figline in 1433 had been diverted from his medical studies by Cosimo in order to learn classics and eventually to take charge of the Platonic Academy. His first great assignment was to translate Plato into Latin; a task that took him until 1477, although it was not generally published for another five years. Devoted philosopher though he was, Ficino's work demonstrates more clearly than that of most of his contemporaries that the Renaissance

was essentially a time for action and not for cerebration. Although a
devout Christian (he took Holy Orders at the age of forty), his confused
Renaissance mind held that the truth of Christianity had to be proved
by reference to the testimony of the sybils of Virgil and of Plato. He
failed to see the inconsistent nature of this proposition. In his *Theologica
Platonica,* his major work, Ficino makes a heroic attempt to bring all
his doctrinal views forward in a systematic whole, but the work lacks
any real unity of purpose or scientific clarity of thought. Although his
entire career was spent in contemplation of philosophical questions
Ficino subscribes to all the prejudices of his time. This was an age still
much influenced by astrology, and Ficino saw nothing incongruous in
explaining his habitual melancholy as being due to the influence of
Saturn. The lasting significance of Ficino's contribution is confined to
the enthusiasm for Platonic studies with which he inspired his students.
But, as in other Renaissance fields, it was the attempt that counted
more than the achievement.

On arrival in Florence, Savonarola was distressed to discover such
wide-spread enthusiasm for Platonic studies. He was equally displeased
at the habitual sarcastic humour to be found among the Florentines
within and without the Convent of San Marco. In the latter respect it
is possible, for once, to have some sympathy with Girolamo. Modern
Florentines still affect a bitingly sarcastic form of wit which seldom
finds favour with other Italians. A twentieth-century Roman, for
example, if faced with a particularly pungent aphorism, will say: 'That
is what a Florentine would say.' Savonarola consistently refused to take
part in the discussions comparing the merits of Platonic and Aristotelean
theories, and in time began to speak increasingly disparagingly of all
literature and learning.

The vehemence of Savonarola's early sermons was thoroughly
unpalatable to the academically-minded citizens whose mild interest in
theology, and whose taste for literary airs and graces, seemed to the
monk to be abominably superficial. There is an account of him preaching
in San Lorenzo in 1483 to audiences which seldom exceeded two score.
At the same time the popular preacher of the day, Mariano de'
Gennazzano, could fill the church of Santo Spirito. Gennazzano was in
the habit of cultivating his audience. He was a favourite of Lorenzo and
greatly praised by Poliziano. In a letter to Tristano Calco written in
April 1489, Poliziano recalled that: 'When he began to speak, I became
wholly absorbed by the sonorous voice, the choice language, the noble
sentences. I marked the periods and the pauses, and was subdued by the
harmonious cadences.'[3] It will be seen that Poliziano enthuses over the

manner of the sermon rather than its matter; a judgement as shallow as Gennazzano's own sermons were: they are now forgotten.

Savonarola did not take kindly to the Florentines' failure to appreciate his orations. In his disappointment he abandoned himself increasingly to religious ecstasy and to frequent repetitions of his watchword: 'Repent and return to the Lord.' For a year or so he moved to San Gimignano and found some temporary peace in the Tuscan countryside; but he was still exclaiming that 'the church will be scourged, then regenerated, and this quickly.' Shortly after that he seems to have met Pico della Mirandola at a meeting of the Dominican Order held at Reggio. The two opposites were immediately attracted by each other. It would be hard to imagine two more different personalities − the haggard, emaciated Savonarola in his monk's robes, and the charming, graceful and sociable Pico. But they shared many philosophical interests and, in 1490, Pico persuaded Lorenzo to recall Savonarola to Florence. Savonarola decided that the time had come to launch a more determined attack on the Florentine butterflies and the way in which they salved their conscience, as he saw it, by flirting with Platonism. His sermons at San Marco on 1 August made more impression than any of his previous orations. He had taken great care to identify in the Bible passages which would confirm his thoughts, inspirations and prophecies, and he demanded the abrogation of Platonism. Before long San Marco became too small to contain the crowds who came to hear him, and Savonarola moved to a larger forum in the Duomo itself. It cannot be imagined that this ascetic crusade was received with any enthusiasm by Lorenzo and his friends. Five leading citizens took it on themselves to advise Savonarola to moderate his sermons, but they met with an indignant response: 'Although I am a stranger, and Lorenzo is not only a citizen but the first among them it is I who will remain, and he who shall leave the city.'[4]

Religious ecstasy had now carried Savonarola to a point of arrogance which he would have been the first to denounce in others. At about the same time as his first confrontation with the Medici advisers, he prophesied that Lorenzo, the Pope and the King of Naples were near their end.

Inspired, as he thought, with a Divine mission, Savonarola continued to preach with what would now be called evangelical eloquence and was elected Prior of San Marco. It was the custom of the Prior to acknowledge the patronage of the head of the Medici family, but this was not all to Savonarola's liking. He refused to pay homage to Lorenzo: 'I regard my election as coming from God alone, and to him I shall pay obeisance.'[5]

Lorenzo did, however, send again for the now discredited Gennazzano with a view to reviving his influence as an antidote to Savonarola, but Gennazzano was no match for the Dominican. In his first sermon – a dissertation which had been prepared with some care – he launched an overt attack on Savonarola's teaching in terms so exaggerated that it was his own reputation which suffered.

Savonarola's influence was growing day by day. The structure of his sermons is strangely simple. It is that followed by nearly all evangelists. First, there is the exposition of a passage from the Bible; then the topical application which, in Savonarola's case, would be declaimed in eloquent and powerful language. The defect in his method was that somewhere in the middle he would ascend to the clouds and lose himself in mystical ideas. His audience could not follow him and the blind mouths which looked up were probably not fed.

In addition to his reputation as a preacher, Savonarola was famed for his extraordinary powers of prediction. He foretold the coming of the French, the expulsion of the Medici and, frequently, even his own violent death. Sometimes his prophecies were based on fairly naive reasoning. A relevant passage of scripture would be selected for the occasion, which would be followed by a melancholy contemplation of the corrupt state of the church and society. From this point it was only a short step to the conclusion that retribution must follow. There is nothing very original in this method; it is common to most seers. At other times he would claim to be inspired by some divine visitation; he was possessed by the Holy Spirit; his prophecies came straight from God whose humble servant, Savonarola, was merely the channel through which these utterances were poured forth for the good of his country. But his own description of his prophetic method was self-contradictory and demonstrates once more the unhappy task of the prophet who tries to rationalise his prophecies:

> I am not either a prophet or the son of a prophet. I do not dare to assume that awful name; but I am certain that the things I announce will come to pass, because they spring from Christian doctrine, from the spirit of evangelical charity.[6]

His prophecies were the more readily received, not only by the more credulous sectors of the populace, because they were still competing with beliefs in magic and the supernatural which were no more susceptible of proof. Savonarola ascribed to religious influence what contemporary philosophers ascribed to occult powers. Even the learned

Ficino changed every day the precious stone which was set in his ring. Guicciardini was convinced that he could speak to supernatural forces; and the scholarly Landino claimed that he had worked out a system for reconciling the future of Christianity with the influence of the stars.

Lorenzo, on his deathbed, sent for Savonarola: 'I know no honest friar but him' — perhaps the final proof of the magnanimity which had marked his whole career. Of the varying versions of Savonarola's reaction, we prefer the Christian charity of Poliziano's description. It would be comforting to assume that this charity also moved Savonarola to grant absolution to the dying Medici.

Savonarola had still six years to live before he was executed at the age of forty-five on 23 May 1498. During this time his rise was rapid; for a time his power was nearly supreme; but his fall was sudden. After Lorenzo's death, the Florentines revolted against his son, Piero, and the Medici were soon driven from Florence. Savonarola, on the other hand, gained prestige, both for being summoned to Lorenzo's deathbed and for the, by now, almost inevitable vindication of his prophecies. Lorenzo had died, as he had foretold, and within the same month the death of Pope Innocent VIII was reported. Inspired by Savonarola's sermons and by the inevitable realisation that the hedonism of Lorenzo and his followers was not enough, the Florentines were abandoning their frivolous practices and giving way to remorse.

In the next few years Savonarola made great progress in removing the luxurious practices which had been prevalent under the Medici. His sermons were given a practical application. Indecent costumes were forbidden; hymns replaced the Carnival songs; public worship was revived; even bankers were said to refund sums of money illegally acquired. But there were still some Florentines who felt uneasy when surrounded by this universal virtue and who jeered at Savonarola's followers as *Piagnoni* (mourners), *Stropiccioni* (sycophants) or *Mastica-paternostri* (chewers of paternosters).

At the height of his powers, in 1497, Savonarola was able to insist on the public burning of all the symbols of vanity. It had become apparent that the youths of Florence under Dolfo Spini were conspiring to ensure that the Carnival should once again be celebrated as in Lorenzo's time. But Savonarola's principal lieutenant, Fra Domenico, organised bands of children to collect throughout the city all the vanities that remained, lewd masks, immodest dresses, musical instruments and scurrilous books, including Boccaccio's *Decamerone* — said to be much favoured by nuns in their cloisters. On the last day of Carnival (7 February) after a solemn religious procession through the city, the vanities were burnt in a huge bonfire in the Piazza. A pyramid had been constructed with eight sides, each of fifteen steps. It measured sixty feet high with a circumference of 240 feet at the base. The holocaust was impressive.

But another kind of conflagration — the abortive trial by fire — was to bring about Savonarola's own downfall a year later in 1498. The primary cause of this macabre event appears to have been the long-standing hostility of the Franciscan monks of Santa Croce to the Dominicans at San Marco. The Franciscans had long been bitter that their more erudite eloquence should be overshadowed by Savonarola's evangelism. The challenge to the ordeal seems to have been first made a year earlier when the Franciscan monk, Fra Francesco da Puglia, offered to undergo it along with the Dominican, Fra Domenico da Pescia, in order to clarify their doctrinal differences. The challenge was renewed in March 1498 when the Signoria actually drew up rules for the ordeal which was to produce a miracle. To our eyes trial by fire has very little to commend it as a method of solving a theological dispute, and the action of the Signoria revealed that superstition and barbarism had survived the humanising influence of the Renaissance.

On 7 April the two rival monks marched in devotional procession to the Piazza but after procedural difficulties, a heavy thunderstorm, and some unseemly squabbles about the part played by Savonarola (the Friar did not offer himself as a candidate for the pyre) the ordeal was called off. The populace, robbed of their spectacle, blamed Savonarola who seemed to have avoided the challenge. On the following day San Marco was attacked by the mob and Savonarola and his two chief supporters were ordered by the Signoria to attend at the Palazzo where before long they were put on trial.

Savonarola's attempt to combine religious and political reform had failed and, ironically, he was first charged with political intrigue leading to treason and with communicating direct with foreign powers. Only after the secular court had condemned him did the Pope's commissioners investigate him on his religious teaching and prophecies. His political, not his religious, enemies secured his ultimate defeat. The trial was marked by the ritual features of the time — torture, forced depositions and the falsification of evidence which, in the case against Savonarola, was unusually blatant. There was little chance of acquittal. Savonarola who had defied and, as he thought, destroyed the humanism of the Medici was to perish by a reversion to barbarism of a kind he had himself condoned. The sentence was confirmed and the three friars were to be hanged and their bodies burned. A platform was built for the purpose in the Piazza facing the Palazzo Vecchio. After they had been stripped of their robes the three Dominicans in order, with Savonarola last, met their end with becoming composure. The ashes were thrown in the Arno.

The conclusion on Savonarola must be that he never properly succeeded in overcoming the religious scepticism and, at times, the utter indifference of the Florentines. Florence reacted to his exhortations first with doubt and then with what appeared to be an almost hysterical belief, and then back to doubt again. He was never accepted on his own terms and his reputation depended not, as he would have wished, on the strength of his religious belief and his powers of oratory, but on the realisation of his prophecies and his identification with the anti-Medici party after the death of Lorenzo. But, as Villari observes, the Renaissance was a time of heroes rather than thinkers and to ask them what their object was, whither they were going – as Savonarola attempted – was a vain question.

Notes

1.   J.A. Symonds, *Renaissance in Italy: The Revival of Learning* (John Murray, London, 1920).
2.   Pasquale Villari, *The History of Girolamo Savonarola and His Times* (Longmans, London, 1863).
3.   Ibid.
4.   Ibid.
5.   Ibid.
6.   Ibid.

EPILOGUE

What remains to record the rule of the Medici throughout the Quattrocento? Some of them remain perpetuated in the paintings of Gozzoli, Botticelli and others, though none of the Medici are preserved in such vivid condition as the frescoes by Pinturicchio in the Baptistery of Siena Cathedral. Their literary works and those of the period are readily available. The Medici rulers lie buried in the family church of San Lorenzo and their supporters are, for the most part, interred in Santa Croce or elsewhere in the city. But tombs and tombstones, however brilliantly executed, are singularly ineffective in recalling past glories. Recollections inspired by sarcophagi or epitaphs are a work of induction by the spectator. In and around Florence, however, are the houses and villas they lived in and, although they are now mainly used for purposes quite different, their presence in Florence, Fiesole and the Mugello valley recalls more than anything else the departed elegance of Giovanni, Cosimo and Lorenzo and the members of their court.

First, in Florence itself, is the Palazzo Medici, which now serves the state as the Office of the Prefecture. It was the family's town house and their basic headquarters from the time it was built to Michelozzo's design starting in 1440 till it was looted at the time of Piero's expulsion in the last decade of the century. Cosimo, it will be recalled, got into trouble for starting so ambitious a construction — although he thought he had chosen an unostentatious design in preferring Michelozzo's plans to those of Brunelleschi. Here the nuptials of Lorenzo and Clarice Orsini were celebrated in all the grandeur of Florentine pageantry. And here, at Lorenzo's dinner table, his mother, Lucrezia Tornabuoni, encouraged Luigi Pulci to recite the latest scabrous stanzas of his *Morgante Maggiore*. The building remained in the possession of the family until it was sold to the Riccardi in 1659 and there is little of Medici history that is not connected with it.

The main feature of the Palazzo, which inspired many similar buildings throughout Florence, including Alberti's Palazzo Strozzi, is the courtyard whose elegant proportions combined with the surrounding columns give an impression of spaciousness entirely novel at the time. Donatello was available to decorate the frieze with a series of roundels and careful reproduction of antique cameos. Later, Gozzoli, in his last commission for the family, was to include their leading figures in his fresco of the

132

Adoration of the Magi. All the Medici Quattrocento is summarised in the stones of this building.

The country house tradition was strong throughout the century. Most leading Florentine families had their villas outside the city and the Medici were no exception. The first villa known to have been owned by them was the Villa Medici at Careggi which was bought by Giovanni de' Bicci in 1417 and later enlarged by Michelozzo at Cosimo's direction. It had been originally designed as a fortified building, and some of this impression remains, despite Michelozzo's delicate work on the windows and the facade — a reminder that siege or ambush were never far away. Poliziano first took refuge in the Villa when he was expelled from the Medici household by Clarice. Ficino was often to be found here, along with the other Platonists who enjoyed Lorenzo's hospitality. Lorenzo commissioned Verrocchio's *Boy with the Dolphin* for the courtyard, and it was here he was brought in his last illness. This, though not the favourite, was the principal Medici country house.

Caffagiuolo, a greater distance from Florence at the head of the Mugello valley, is a gloomy building. It seems to have been intended as a last place of retreat, and Clarice, her family, and Poliziano found their exile there almost unbearable. Wet, cold and gloomy, no one would stay in it longer than necessary. Nearby is the formidable tower known as *Il Trebbio,* also fortress-like in character, which must have served as a base for hawking expeditions. Falconry was much practised by the Florentines. But the Medici had few happy memories of Caffagiuolo.

The Villa Medici at Fiesole was originally built for Cosimo's second son, Giovanni, and was completed about 1461, three years before Cosimo's death. It was the nearest of the villas to Florence and, consequently, in frequent use. Architecturally, Michelozzo's design is of great interest for his skilful use of the terrain. The villa lies against the hill slope and all the domestic offices, the cellars and the stables are placed under the villa itself. Poliziano was eventually allowed to stay here after his quarrel with Clarice, and it was in these surroundings that he started one of his most important works of classical scholarship — the *Sylvae.*

Lorenzo loved best of all the Villa Ambra at Poggio a Caiano where he found all the quintessence of the Tuscan countryside. The original date of the villa is doubtful, but at one time it had belonged to the Strozzi and then to the Rucellai families and, in 1480, when he looked forward to a long period of peaceful rule, Lorenzo enlisted Giuliano da Sangallo to adapt it to his wishes. Poliziano wrote in praise of life at the villa, and the interior walls are covered with some interesting frescoes.

The first ones seem to have been done by Filippino Lippi, while others of less distinguished origin recall scenes of family history. This is a not uncommon feature of Italian villas: other examples can be seen in the Villa Medici at Rome and at Caprarola, not far from the city.

All the Medici villas, except perhaps Caffagiuolo, have their own elegance. They are still imbued with the spirit of the great family who ruled throughout the Quattrocento.

SELECTED BIBLIOGRAPHY

Acton, Harold *The Last Medici*, 1932; rev. edn, 1958; reprinted, 1973.

Ady, Cecilia M. *Lorenzo de' Medici and Renaissance Italy*, 1955.

Allen, Eric *The Story of Lorenzo the Magnificent*, 1961.

Antal, Friedrich *Florentine Painting and its Social Background*, 1948.

Armstrong, E. *Lorenzo de' Medici*, 1896.

Barzini, Luigi *The Italians*, 1964.

Baxandall, Michael *Painting and Experience in XVth Century Italy*, 1972.

Berenson, Bernard *Florentine Painters of the Renaissance*, 1909.

Biagi, Guido *The Private Life of the Renaissance Florentines*, 1896.

Boccalaro, Mario A. *Angelo Poliziano, Il Poeta del Bel Canto*, 1951.

Borsook, Eve *The Companion Guide to Florence*, 1966.

Brinton, Selwyn *The Golden Age of the Medici*, 1925.

Burckhardt, Jacob *The Civilisation of the Renaissance in Italy*, trans. S.G.C. Middlemore; new edn, 1958.

Burke, Peter *Culture and Society in Renaissance Italy*, 1972.

Castiglione, Baldassare *The Book of the Courtier*, new edn, 1956.

Chamberlin, E.R. *Everyday life in Renaissance Times*, 1965.

Collinson-Morley, L. *The Early Medici*, 1935.

Cronin, Vincent *The Florentine Renaissance*, 1967.

Cruttwell, M. *Verrocchio*, 1904.

Dami, Brunetto *Giovanni Bicci de' Medici*, 1899.

Ehrman, S.H. *Three Renaissance Silhouettes*, 1928.

Elyot, Sir Thomas *The Boke named the Governor*, ed. H.H.S. Croft, 1880.

Ewart, K.D. *Cosimo de' Medici*, 1889.

Ficino, Marsilio *Letters*, Vol. I; trans. School of Economic Science, London, 1973.

Gadol, Joan *Leon Batista Alberti; Universal Man of the Early Renaissance*, 1969.

Gage, John *Life in Italy at the Time of the Medici*, 1968.

Gill, Joseph *The Council of Florence*, 1959.

Gombrich, E.H. *The Story of Art*, 1956.

    Symbolic Images, 1972.

Guicciardini, Francesco *History of Italy*, new edn, 1966.

Gutkind, Curt S. *Cosimo de' Medici: Pater Patriae*, 1938.

Hale, J.R. *Machiavelli and Renaissance Italy*, 1961.

Horsburgh, E.L.S. *Girolamo Savonarola*, 1901.

Jacob, E.F. (ed.) *Italian Renaissance Studies*, 1960.

Janson, H.W. *The Sculpture of Donatello*, 1957.

Jesup, E. *The Lives of Picus and Pascal*, 1723.

Kristeller, P.O. *The Classics and Renaissance Thought*, 1955.

Laven, Peter *Renaissance Italy, 1464–1534*, 1966.

McCarthy, Mary *The Stones of Florence*, 1959.

Machiavelli, Niccolo *Discourses*, trans. L.J. Walker, 1950.

　Il Principe, ed. L.A. Burd, 1891.

Maguire, Yvonne *The Private Life of Lorenzo the Magnificent*, 1936.
　The Women of the Medici, 1927.

Masson, Georgina, *Italian Villas and Palaces*, 1959.

Moorehead, Alan *The Villa Diana*, 1953.

More, Sir Thomas *The Life of John Picus, Earl of Mirandola, 1510*, reprinted with a study by J. Rigg, 1890.

Murray, Peter *The Art of the Renaissance*, 1969.

Pater, Walter *The Renaissance*, 1910.

Politian and Tasso *The Orpheus and Aminta*, trans. with an essay by L.E. Lord, 1931.

Pope-Hennessy, John *Italian High Renaissance and Baroque Sculpture*, 1963.

Ridolfi, Roberto *The Life of Francesco Guiccardini*, trans. C. Grayson, 1967.
　The Life of Girolamo Savonarola, trans. C. Grayson, 1963.

Robb, N. *Neoplatonism of the Italian Renaissance*, 1935.

Roover, Raymond de *The Rise and Decline of the Medici Bank, 1397–1494*, 1963.

Roscoe, W. *Life of Lorenzo de' Medici*, 1872.

Ross, Janet *Lives of the Early Medici as told in their Correspondence*, 1910.

Rubinstein, Nicolai *The Government of Florence under the Medici 1434–1494*, 1968.

Rubinstein, Nicolai (ed.) *Florentine Studies; Politics and Society in Renaissance Florence*, 1968.

Schevill, Ferdinand *The Medici*, 1950.

Smeaton, Oliphant *The Medici and the Italian Renaissance*, 1901.

Smollett, Tobias *Travels through France and Italy*, 1766.

Symonds, J.A. *The Renaissance in Italy: The Revival of Learning*, 1920.

Vasari, Giorgio *The Lives of the Artists*, trans. George Bull, 1965.

Vespasiano da Bisticci *Lives (The Vespasiano Memoirs)*, trans. W.G. and

E. Waters, 1926.
Villari, Pasquale *The History of Girolamo Savonarola and His Times,*
 1863.
Weiss, Roberto *The Spread of Italian Humanism,* 1964.
Young, G.F. *The Medici,* 1909.

INDEX

A Thornhill Guide 5

Hillwalking in Scotland

By RICHARD F. GILBERT

The Fannichs

A THORNHILL GUIDE

First published in 1979 by
Thornhill Press Ltd
24 Moorend Road
Cheltenham

ISBN 0 904110 75 3

2nd Edition June 1979

This book is an enlarged edition of the original guide *Hill Walking in Scotland*, published in 1976 and now out of print.

Printed by
R. J. Washington
Southwood Lane
Cheltenham